THE *Sunset*
CASSEROLE BOOK

**By the editors
of Sunset Books
and Sunset Magazine**

LANE BOOKS · MENLO PARK, CALIFORNIA

About Casseroles

Every manner of cook can find a place in her (or his) repertoire for a good casserole recipe. Casseroles are the delight of the hostess, the busy housewife, the young bride, the bachelor chef, the working wife—in short, of anyone who wishes to serve delicious meals without a flurry of last-minute preparation.

Casserole dishes may be inexpensive or expensive, simple or complicated. Many of them can be prepared on the spur of the moment from ingredients found on most kitchen shelves. But there are three endearing qualities that all of them have in common: They can be prepared ahead of time; they will cook without constant supervision; and they can be served quickly and easily to any number of people.

Once a casserole is in the oven, the cook can sit down and enjoy the pre-dinner hour with her guests or family until it is time to whisk the casserole to the table. Accompaniments can be simple: a crisp green salad, a crusty hot bread or rolls, a favorite wine. In some instances, the casserole itself is designed to be the accompaniment to a simple roasted or barbecued or grilled meat.

Casseroles can, and should, be served right in their cooking containers. The wonderful sizes, shapes, and colors of the baking dishes themselves add decoration to a dinner table or buffet. Collecting casserole dishes can even become a hobby in itself. The more you cook with casseroles, the more often you will find yourself looking for new and unusual ones to add to your collection.

The casserole recipes that appear in this book are favorites of the Sunset food editors. They have been selected as the very *best* of the vast number of excellent casserole recipes that have been prepared in the Sunset kitchens, passed by exacting taste panels, and published in Sunset Magazine. We hope they'll provide enjoyment for you and your family and your guests.

Contents

Beef cubes and small whole onions, in about equal proportions, are the base for the Favorite Meat Casserole on page 6. You don't have to brown the meat before cooking.

Meat Casseroles

Hearty main dishes and one-dish meals

Beef Casserole, Mexican Style

This hearty casserole is full of meat and richly seasoned.

2 pounds round steak or chuck roast
1 clove garlic, minced or mashed
¼ teaspoon pepper
2 tablespoons chili powder
2 tablespoons prepared mustard
1 medium-sized onion, chopped
2 tablespoons salad oil
2 tablespoons butter
1 can (7 oz.) pitted ripe olives
½ cup uncooked regular rice
1 large can (1 lb., 12 oz.) tomatoes
1 can (1 lb.) red kidney beans
1 bouillon cube
¾ cup boiling water
1 teaspoon paprika

Spread meat with a mixture of garlic, pepper, 1 tablespoon of the chili powder, and the prepared mustard. Cut it into 1-inch squares. Sauté the onion in salad oil and butter until golden. Slice ¾ of olives; leave remainder whole. Make a layer of half the meat in bottom of a 3-quart casserole. Cover with half the sautéed onions. Sprinkle with half the rice, tomatoes, and sliced olives. Repeat layers. Top with the beans to which has been added the remaining 1 tablespoon chili powder. Dissolve bouillon cube in boiling water, pour over to almost cover. Sprinkle with paprika; arrange whole olives on top. Bake uncovered in a moderate oven (350°) for about 2 hours, adding more bouillon as needed. Makes 8 servings.

Round Steak and Vegetable Casserole

This hearty beef and vegetable casserole could be the hot entrée for a picnic lunch or supper. Bundle it in newspapers to keep it warm until serving time, or carry it in one of the many insulated picnic containers now on the market.

2 to 3 pounds round steak, cut in
    serving-size pieces
2 tablespoons salad oil
2 large onions, sliced
2 cups sliced carrots
2 cups sliced fresh mushrooms
1 medium-sized green pepper, sliced
½ pound fresh green beans, cut in pieces
3 tomatoes, peeled and sliced
½ cup uncooked regular rice
2 teaspoons salt
1½ teaspoons sweet basil
¼ teaspoon freshly ground black pepper
1 cup shredded Cheddar cheese

Brown the meat in oil in a large frying pan. Arrange one-third of the sliced vegetables in a 4-quart casserole. Place half of the meat pieces over these vegetables and sprinkle with one-third of the rice and seasonings. Add another third of the sliced vegetables, the remaining meat, one-third of the seasonings, and all of the remaining rice. Top with the remaining sliced vegetables and seasonings.

Cover and bake the casserole in a moderate oven (350°) for 1½ hours, or until the meat is tender. Remove the cover, sprinkle the cheese over the vegetables and return the casserole to the oven to melt the cheese. Makes 6 to 8 servings.

Favorite Meat Casserole

This beef casserole is especially easy to prepare. The cubes of stew meat do not have to be browned before you combine them with the onions and seasonings.

2 pounds boneless beef stew meat,
   cut in about 1½-inch cubes
About 16 onions (same size as meat pieces)
4 whole cloves
2 tablespoons sugar
1 cup water
1½ teaspoons salt
½ teaspoon brown bottled gravy sauce
1 tablespoon red wine vinegar
1 bay leaf
⅛ teaspoon thyme
2 tablespoons flour blended
   with 2 tablespoons water

In a greased 2-quart casserole, alternate the meat pieces and onions (if larger onions are used, cut into halves or quarters—you should have about same number as meat pieces). Stick cloves into onions. In a frying pan, heat the sugar, stirring until melted and caramelized to a dark golden brown (not burned). Remove from heat, add the water, then stir again over the heat until the sugar has redissolved. Stir in the salt, gravy sauce, vinegar, bay leaf, and thyme. Pour over meat in casserole.

Cover and bake in a moderately slow oven (325°) until the meat is tender, 2 to 3 hours. Blend the flour and water and stir into the meat gravy about 15 minutes before serving it. Continue cooking until thickened. Makes about 6 servings.

Steak and Navy Bean Casserole

Generous portions of meat flavor this bean casserole of Scottish origin. It is hearty fare, and very full-flavored—wonderful for picnics and camping trips as well as for family suppers.

2 pounds round steak, cut in 1-inch cubes
2 tablespoons shortening or salad oil
2 cups cooked (but still firm) navy beans
1 can (1 lb.) tomatoes (2 cups)
Salt and pepper to taste
2 cups sliced onions
½ cup brown sugar, firmly packed
5 slices bacon

In a large frying pan, cook round steak in shortening until browned on both sides. Add beans, tomatoes, and salt and pepper to taste. Cover and simmer for 10 minutes. Spoon half of this mixture into a 2-quart casserole. Spread onions over the bean mixture, then sprinkle with half the brown sugar. Add remaining half of bean mixture, sprinkle with remaining sugar. Lay strips of bacon over the top. Bake, uncovered, in a moderately slow oven (325°) for about 1 hour. Makes 6 servings.

Casserole in Six Layers

Canned mixed vegetable juices give this meat and vegetable combination a particularly good flavor.

2 cups sliced raw potatoes
2 cups sliced celery
1 pound ground beef
1 large green pepper, finely chopped
2 teaspoons salt
1 teaspoon monosodium glutamate
1 can (12 oz.) mixed vegetable juices
Green pepper slices for garnish

In a greased 2-quart casserole, arrange layers of potatoes, celery, ground beef, and green pepper, seasoning with salt and monosodium glutamate. Pour over vegetable juices. Garnish with green pepper slices. Cover and bake in a moderate oven (350°) for 1½ to 2 hours; remove cover for the last 30 minutes. Makes 6 servings.

Beef Burgundy

Here's an entrée to add to your repertoire of company meals. You can make it early in the day, refrigerate it, and heat it in the oven while you enjoy yourself with your guests.

16 small white onions, peeled (about 1 pound)
6 strips lean bacon, diced
¼ cup (⅛ lb.) butter or margarine
4 pounds beef chuck, cut in 1½-inch cubes, fat trimmed off
¼ cup brandy (optional)
1½ teaspoons salt
¼ teaspoon freshly ground pepper
2 cups Burgundy or other dry red table wine
2 whole cloves garlic, peeled
2 cups small whole or sliced fresh mushrooms
1½ cups water
1 or 2 sprigs parsley
1 celery top
1 carrot, quartered
1 bay leaf
1 sprig fresh thyme or 1 teaspoon dried thyme
6 tablespoons flour
½ cup cold water

Brown onions with bacon and butter in a Dutch oven; remove onions and bacon with a slotted spoon and set aside. Add meat to pan and brown well on all sides. If desired, pour brandy over beef and set aflame, tilting pan to keep flame going as long as possible. Sprinkle meat with salt and pepper. Add Burgundy, garlic, mushrooms, the 1½ cups water, onions, and bacon. Make a bouquet garni by tying together in a piece of cheesecloth the parsley, celery top, carrot, bay leaf, and thyme (use a long string so bouquet can easily be removed from pan). Add bouquet garni. Cover and simmer for about 1½ hours, or until the meat is tender.

Lift beef, mushrooms, and onions out of the pan with a slotted spoon; arrange in a covered 3-quart casserole or baking dish. Strain the liquid through a sieve, discarding bouquet garni, garlic, and bacon. Mix flour to a smooth paste with the ½ cup cold water; stir into meat stock and cook, stirring, until gravy is thick and smooth. Pour gravy over meat and serve immediately, or refrigerate and reheat, covered, in a moderate oven (350°) for about 35 minutes, or until hot and bubbly. Makes 8 to 10 servings.

Beef Burgundy, simplified version of traditional French Boeuf Bourguignonne, is easy-to-serve buffet entrée.

Beef and Olive Casserole

Serve this casserole as a one-dish meal, with crusty sourdough French bread and a simple dessert of fresh fruit and cookies.

2 pounds beef chuck, cut in good-sized cubes
½ cup flour
1 teaspoon salt
Pepper
½ teaspoon marjoram
2 tablespoons shortening
1 pound small white onions, peeled
8 to 10 tiny carrots, scraped
2 cans (10½ oz. each) beef bouillon
1 cup pimiento-stuffed green olives, drained
Butter
Flour

Dust beef with a mixture of the flour, salt, pepper, and marjoram. Brown meat on all sides in the shortening, and put in a 2-quart casserole with the onions and carrots. Add bouillon, cover, and bake in a moderate oven (350°) for about 1½ hours, or until meat and vegetables are almost tender. Add olives and continue baking for another 20 minutes, or until very tender. Pour off juices and thicken slightly with a little kneaded butter and flour (1 tablespoon of each for each cup of sauce). Makes about 6 servings.

Beef and Cheese Strata

A Sunday night supper is a likely occasion for this custard-like casserole.

8 slices white bread
Butter or margarine
1 jar (5 oz.) dried beef
2 cups shredded sharp Cheddar cheese
4 eggs, beaten
2¼ cups milk

Remove crusts from bread; lightly butter one side of each slice. Place 4 slices, buttered side up, in bottom of a greased 8-inch square baking dish. Separate dried beef and arrange half of it over the bread. Sprinkle 1 cup of the cheese over the beef. Add one more layer of the dried beef and top with remaining cheese. Place the last 4 slices of bread, buttered side up, on top. Combine eggs and milk and pour over bread; allow to stand for 1 hour or longer. Bake, uncovered, in a moderate oven (350°) for 1 hour or until puffed, brown, and set. Makes 4 generous servings.

Shortribs with Limas

This substantial casserole combines flavorful meat with canned dried limas.

3 pounds beef shortribs, cut in serving-size pieces
Salt and pepper to taste
2 tablespoons shortening or salad oil
1 medium-sized onion, sliced
½ cup brown sugar, firmly packed
1 teaspoon dry mustard
1 tablespoon flour
2 tablespoons vinegar
2 tablespoons lemon juice
¼ teaspoon grated lemon peel
1 bay leaf
1½ cups water
2 cans (1 lb. each) cooked, dried limas, drained

Sprinkle shortribs lightly with salt and pepper. In a large heavy frying pan, heat shortening; add ribs and brown on all sides. Remove the ribs to a large casserole or baking pan (about 9 by 13 by 3 inches). Using the same fat in the frying pan, sauté onion until golden brown; remove from pan and set aside. To the pan add brown sugar, mustard, flour, vinegar, lemon juice, and lemon peel, stirring until blended. Stir in water and bring to a boil; pour over meat. Bake, uncovered, in a hot oven (400°) for about 1¼ hours. Stir in limas; top with onions. Cover and continue baking for ½ hour. Makes 6 to 8 servings.

Round Steak en Casserole

In this one-dish meal, the browned round steak is laid on a bed of onions; then potatoes, carrots, and peas are heaped on top.

4 onions, sliced
3 tablespoons butter or margarine
1½ pounds round steak, cut in serving-size pieces
Water
2 tablespoons finely chopped parsley
2 teaspoons salt
¼ teaspoon pepper
¼ teaspoon thyme
¼ teaspoon marjoram
4 medium-sized potatoes, cut in 1-inch cubes
1 cup sliced carrots
1 package (10 oz.) frozen peas, thawed

Sauté onions in butter until golden brown; arrange onions in the bottom of a 2½-quart casserole. Cut fat from meat and rub over frying pan if additional fat is needed. Brown meat quickly on both sides; place in casserole on top of onions. Pour about ¼ cup water into drippings, stir, then pour over onions and meat; add just enough more water to cover onion layer. Sprinkle parsley, salt, pepper, thyme, and marjoram over meat; arrange potato cubes on top. Cover and bake in a slow oven (300°) for 1 hour. Arrange carrots and peas over potatoes, and continue baking in a slow oven for 1 hour, or until meat is tender. Makes 6 servings.

Casserole of Beef

This dish follows the familiar stew pattern, but it has a unique character. The long cooking time allows the flavors to blend and mellow.

4 strips bacon
2 pounds round steak, cut ½ inch thick
¼ cup flour
2 tablespoons salad oil
1 large clove garlic, peeled
⅔ cup boiling water
⅔ cup red wine or beef bouillon
½ teaspoon salt
6 small boiling onions, peeled
2 cups diced carrots
6 whole black peppers
6 whole cloves
2 bay leaves

Cook bacon in frying pan until light brown, but not crisp. Drain and cut into 1-inch pieces. Cut beef into 1-inch pieces; dredge in flour and brown in salad oil with garlic. Remove garlic; add water, wine, and salt; bring to a boil. Turn the mixture into a 2-quart casserole; add onions, carrots, whole peppers, cloves, bay leaves, and bacon. Cover and bake in a moderately slow oven (325°) about 2 hours. Makes 6 generous servings.

Chinese Style Hamburger Hash

Soy sauce, rice, sliced celery, and crisp fried noodles give the Oriental flavor to this simple ground beef casserole.

1 pound ground beef
2 tablespoons salad oil or shortening
2 medium-sized onions, chopped
1 cup sliced celery
1 can (10½ oz.) mushroom soup
1 can (10½ oz.) cream of chicken soup
1½ cups warm water
½ cup uncooked rice
¼ cup soy sauce
¼ teaspoon pepper
1 can (3 oz.) crisp chow mein noodles

Brown meat in oil until slightly crumbly. Add onions, celery, mushroom and chicken soups, and warm water. Stir in rice, soy sauce, and pepper. Turn into a lightly greased casserole (about 2-quart size). Cover and bake in a moderate oven (350°) for 30 minutes; remove cover and continue baking for 30 minutes longer. Cover the mixture with the crisp chow mein noodles and continue baking for 15 minutes more. Makes 8 servings.

Macaroni Beef Casserole

This is a good casserole to serve to a group of teen-agers. If you make this dish ahead, cover and reheat in a slow oven (300°).

2 pounds ground beef
1 medium-sized onion, chopped
½ cup (¼ lb.) butter or margarine
1 package (8 oz.) macaroni, cooked and drained
¼ cup catsup
¼ cup beef bouillon, white wine, or water
1 cup shredded Cheddar cheese
⅓ cup chopped parsley
½ teaspoon pepper
½ teaspoon cinnamon
3 teaspoons salt
⅓ cup flour
2½ cups milk
1 teaspoon dry mustard
3 eggs, slightly beaten

Sauté ground beef and onion in 2 tablespoons of the butter until browned and crumbly. Combine with the cooked macaroni, catsup, bouillon, ½ cup of the cheese, parsley, pepper, cinnamon, and 2 teaspoons of the salt. Turn into a greased 13 by 9 by 3-inch baking pan. Heat remaining 6 tablespoons butter; add flour and cook until bubbly. Gradually stir in milk. Add remaining 1 teaspoon salt and mustard and cook, stirring, until thickened. Gradually stir the hot mixture into eggs. Pour into the casserole. Sprinkle with remaining ½ cup cheese. Bake, uncovered, in a moderate oven (350°) for about 30 minutes; let stand for about 15 minutes before serving. Makes 8 to 10 servings.

Meat Ball and Rice Casserole

This recipe will appeal especially to those cooks who like to season with a combination of herbs.

1 cup uncooked regular rice
1 large can (1 lb., 12 oz.) tomatoes
1 tablespoon shortening
1½ teaspoons salt
½ teaspoon dried rosemary or
   2 sprigs fresh rosemary
¼ teaspoon crumbled dried sage
   or 1 sprig fresh sage
1 pound ground beef
1½ teaspoons salt
½ teaspoon pepper
¼ teaspoon powdered savory
1 egg, slightly beaten
½ cup fine dry bread crumbs
¼ cup milk
2 tablespoons shortening
½ cup shredded Cheddar cheese

Combine rice, broken-up tomatoes, shortening, salt, rosemary, and sage in top of double boiler. Heat to boiling point, stirring occasionally, then cover and cook over boiling water until rice is done, about 25 minutes.

Meanwhile, mix together ground beef, salt, pepper, savory, egg, bread crumbs, and milk. Form into balls about the size of golf balls. Fry in melted shortening until brown on all sides. Turn rice into greased 2-quart casserole, place meat balls on top, and sprinkle with cheese. Bake, uncovered, in a moderate oven (350°) for 20 minutes. Makes 8 servings with 3 meat balls apiece.

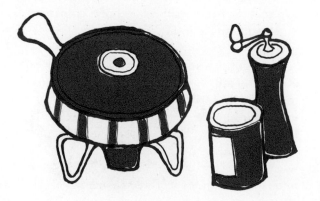

Parmesan-glazed biscuits surround browned beef, mushrooms, artichoke hearts in Beef Pot Pie.

Beef Pot Pie

The kind of deep and rich flavor you find in this beef pie can be achieved only by long slow cooking.

2 pounds round steak, cut in 1-inch cubes
Salt and pepper
Flour
4 tablespoons olive oil or salad oil
2 tablespoons butter
4 cloves garlic, unpeeled
1 pound mushrooms, cut in halves
1 can (4 oz.) green chilies, seeded and minced
¼ teaspoon marjoram
½ teaspoon dill weed
1 cup red table wine or beef consommé
1 tablespoon wine vinegar
2 cups cooked artichoke bottoms (or hearts)
Parmesan biscuit crust (below)

Sprinkle meat with salt and pepper; roll in flour. In a large heavy frying pan combine oil and butter with garlic. Brown meat. Set meat aside, and discard garlic. Add mushrooms to pan; cover and simmer for about 7 minutes. Add chilies. Return meat to pan; add marjoram, dill weed, wine, and vinegar; cover and simmer very slowly for 1½ hours, stirring occasionally. Add artichokes. Pour this mixture into a deep 2 to 2½-quart casserole.

Top with Parmesan biscuits and bake in a hot oven (400°) for 10 to 15 minutes, or until biscuits are well browned. Makes 6 servings.

Parmesan biscuit crust:

Separate 1 package (8 oz.) refrigerator biscuits; dip each biscuit in melted butter and roll in shredded Parmesan cheese. Place on top of meat and sprinkle lightly with dill weed.

Tamale Pie with Tortillas

Your family may prefer this dish to the usual version of tamale pie.

2 pounds beef chuck, diced
1 tablespoon shortening or salad oil
1 small onion, chopped
1 clove garlic, minced or mashed
1½ teaspoons salt
⅛ teaspoon marjoram
1 tablespoon flour
1 can (10 oz.) red chili sauce
2 cups water
½ cup raisins
1 can (2¼ oz.) sliced ripe olives, drained
Shortening or salad oil for frying
1 package (1 dozen) corn tortillas

Sauté beef in the 1 tablespoon shortening. Add onion, garlic, salt, and marjoram, and cook for 5 minutes. Stir in flour, then gradually stir in chili sauce and water. Cover and simmer until tender. Stir in the raisins and olives.

In another pan, heat ½ inch of shortening. Dip each tortilla in hot fat, then in the hot chili mixture; arrange in a 9 by 13-inch baking dish overlapping 5 on bottom and extending up both ends, and 2 on each side. Fill with chili, saving out ½ cup of the liquid. Top with remaining 3 tortillas. Lap side and end tortillas over top. Moisten top with chili liquid. Bake, uncovered, in a moderately slow oven (325°) for 30 minutes. Makes 8 servings.

Meat Loaf-Vegetable Pie

The "crust" of this deep-dish pie is a curry-seasoned meat loaf. The filling is a combination of eggplant, hominy, and a generous amount of chopped ripe olives.

1 medium-sized eggplant, peeled
    and cut in 1-inch cubes
Boiling salted water
1½ pounds ground beef
1 medium-sized onion, finely chopped
1 egg
2 teaspoons salt
½ teaspoon curry powder
Dash of garlic salt
2 cans (1 lb. each) golden hominy, drained
1 can (4½ oz.) chopped ripe olives
2 tablespoons butter or margarine
1 cup (¼ lb.) shredded Cheddar cheese

Cook eggplant in about 1 cup of boiling salted water for 4 minutes; drain. Mix together the ground meat, half of the chopped onion, the egg, 1 teaspoon of the salt, curry powder, and garlic salt; use two-thirds of the meat mixture to line a greased 2-quart, round casserole.

Mix the parboiled eggplant with the remaining chopped onion, the drained hominy, chopped olives, the other 1 teaspoon salt, and butter cut in bits. Spoon this mixture over the meat loaf lining in the casserole. With a rolling pin, roll out the remaining meat mixture on waxed paper and place over the meat and vegetable pie, pinching the edges of the meat lining and top "crust" together. Sprinkle the top with cheese.

Cover and bake in a hot oven (400°) for 45 minutes; remove cover and continue baking 15 minutes longer, or until nicely browned. Makes 6 to 8 servings.

Stuffed Pepper Casserole

You cut red and green peppers in quarters and line a casserole with their alternating colors for this handsome stuffed pepper entrée.

2 red bell peppers, quartered and seeded
2 green bell peppers, quartered and seeded
1 cup water
½ teaspoon salt
1 pound ground beef
1 tablespoon salad oil or olive oil
1 large onion, chopped
4 slices stale bread
Salt and pepper to taste

Parboil red and green peppers in the 1 cup water with the ½ teaspoon salt for 5 minutes. Lift out pepper quarters, drain well (reserve the cooking water). Place peppers in a greased shallow baking dish (about 9 inches square), alternating the red and green quarters.

Brown meat in oil; add onion and cook until the meat is crumbly and onion is transparent. Break bread into very small pieces and add to browned meat and onions. Season with salt and pepper. Mix in enough of the cooking liquid from the peppers to moisten the bread. Spoon into the pepper shells. Bake, uncovered, in a moderate oven (350°) for 20 minutes. Makes 4 servings.

Forgotten Shortribs

You can put this meat dish in the oven and forget about it most of the day. The shortribs accumulate a delicious, slow-baked flavor as they cook. You might want to serve the rich sauce over hot cooked rice, noodles, or mashed potatoes.

About 1½ teaspoons salt
About ½ teaspoon pepper
3 to 4 pounds beef shortribs
1 can (8 oz.) tomato sauce
2 tablespoons molasses
2 tablespoons cider vinegar
1 teaspoon liquid smoke flavoring
1 tablespoon instant minced onion

Sprinkle salt and pepper on all sides of the shortribs and put into a Dutch oven or 3-quart casserole. In a small pan, combine the tomato sauce with the molasses, vinegar, liquid smoke, and instant minced onion; bring to a boil and simmer for 5 minutes. Pour over the shortribs; cover and bake in a slow oven (275°) for 3 to 4 hours, or until very tender. Just before serving, spoon off any excess fat. (If you prepare this dish a day ahead, refrigerate it, and then lift off the solidified fat before you reheat it.) Makes 4 servings.

Eggplant and Ground Beef Bake

Circles of eggplant mark off the servings in this baked vegetable and meat dish The flavors of both the beef and the eggplant are distinct in this combination.

1 medium-sized eggplant, cut
   in ½-inch-thick slices
Salt
2 tablespoons butter or margarine
½ pound ground beef
1 tablespoon parsley
½ small onion, chopped
¼ teaspoon pepper
½ teaspoon salt
2 tomatoes, peeled and sliced
½ cup water

Sprinkle eggplant lightly with salt and let stand a few minutes; then pat dry. Sauté in melted butter on both sides until golden brown. Remove from pan and set aside. Brown meat in the same pan, stirring until crumbly. Stir in parsley, onion, pepper, salt, and tomatoes, and cook until flavors are blended. In a greased 9-inch square baking pan, put a layer of half the sautéed eggplant, then the meat sauce, and then the remaining eggplant. Stir the water into the drippings in the pan and pour over. Bake, uncovered, in a moderate oven (350°) for 35 minutes, or until the eggplant is tender. Makes 4 servings.

Beefsteak Pie

This pie is English in origin, but this version is richer in mushrooms and has a touch of red wine added for additional flavoring. You can make the pie the day before and store it unbaked in the refrigerator until about 1½ hours before you plan to serve dinner.

2½ teaspoons salt
¼ teaspoon pepper
1 teaspoon *fines herbes* (combination of thyme, oregano, sage, rosemary, marjoram, and basil)
6 tablespoons flour
2½ pounds top sirloin, cut in 1½-inch cubes
1 pound mushrooms, sliced
4 tablespoons (⅛ pound) butter
¼ cup dry red table wine
Egg pastry (recipe below)
1 beaten egg

Combine salt, pepper, herbs, and flour and dredge meat cubes in the mixture. Brown mushrooms in butter over medium heat, stirring, until limp. Arrange half of the beef cubes in the bottom of a 2-quart casserole. Arrange half the mushrooms over the beef and the remaining half of the beef over the mushrooms. On top, make an even layer of the remaining mushrooms. Pour the red wine evenly over.

On a floured board, roll the pastry to make a thick round about ½ inch thick and trim to fit the casserole top. Roll out the pastry trimmings and cut a long strip of dough about ¾ inch in diameter to fit the rim of the casserole. Moisten the edges of the casserole and press the pastry strip onto the rim. Arrange the pastry round over the filling and rim, moisten edges and press to flute, and fasten firmly onto the dough-topped casserole rim.

Roll out any remaining scraps of dough and cut out leaf-shaped ovals to use for decoration. Prick pastry top, brush with beaten egg, arrange the leaf shapes on pastry to decorate and brush again with beaten egg. Bake in a moderate oven (350°) for about 60 minutes or until meat is tender. You can test the meat with a long wooden skewer or knitting needle carefully probed through the pastry. If the top begins to brown too much, cover with brown paper or foil to finish baking. Makes about 6 servings.

Beefsteak Pie has a savory meat and mushroom filling topped with egg-rich pastry; decorations are of the same pastry rolled thin and cut into leaf shapes.

Egg pastry:
1½ cups unsifted flour
½ teaspoon salt
½ cup (¼ pound) butter
1 egg, slightly beaten
4 to 5 tablespoons milk

Put flour into a bowl; stir in salt. Cut in butter until mixture resembles fine crumbs. Add egg and milk, mixing with a fork until dough holds together in a ball. Chill. Roll out as directed above.

Dried Beef and Lima Bean Bake

This colorful combination of dried beef and lima beans is moist enough so it won't dry out too much when reheated. If it appears that some members of the family may be late for dinner, you can put the mixture in individual ramekins and bake or reheat each as needed.

Hot water
1 jar (5 oz.) dried beef, shredded
1 medium-sized onion, finely chopped
1 tablespoon butter or margarine
1 can (1 lb.) lima beans
¼ teaspoon curry powder
¼ pound (1 cup) shredded Cheddar cheese
4 hard-cooked eggs, cut in eighths
1 can (10½ oz.) mushroom soup

Pour hot water over dried beef to remove excess saltiness; drain. Sauté onion in butter until limp; then mix onion with dried beef, lima beans, curry powder, cheese, and eggs. Turn mixture into a greased 1-quart casserole; spoon over mushroom soup. Bake, uncovered, in a moderate oven (350°) for 30 minutes, or until sizzling hot (20 minutes if you are using small casseroles). Makes 6 servings.

Saltimbocca in Casserole

Here's a casserole version of this well-known Italian veal and ham dish.

2 veal round steaks, cut about ½ inch thick (about 1 lb.)
10 to 12 very thin slices prosciutto (about ⅛ lb.)
2 tablespoons butter or olive oil (or 1 tablespoon of each)
1 whole clove garlic
¼ cup dry white wine
1 package (10 oz.) frozen chopped spinach, thawed and drained
¼ teaspoon salt

Trim fat, bone, and connective tissue from veal steaks. Place veal between sheets of waxed paper and pound with a flat-surfaced mallet until ¼ to ⅜ inch thick. Cut in 10 to 12 pieces of fairly even size. Top each piece with a slightly smaller piece of prosciutto. Roll veal around ham and fasten with skewers.

Heat butter or olive oil in a frying pan with garlic. Add veal rolls and lightly brown on all sides (this takes about 3 minutes). Remove from pan and add wine. Boil rapidly until all of the liquid has evaporated from butter. Discard garlic. Stir in spinach and salt; cook until spinach is heated. Spoon into a 1½-quart casserole; top with veal and juices. Cover and bake in moderate oven (350°) for 15 minutes. Makes 3 to 4 servings.

Veal and Pork Casserole

Cream-style corn and corn flakes make a colorful, crunchy topping on this casserole.

¼ cup (⅛ lb.) butter or margarine
½ pound veal stew meat, cut in 1-inch cubes
½ pound pork shoulder, cut in 1-inch cubes
1 teaspoon salt
¼ teaspoon pepper
4 stalks celery, sliced
1 green pepper, seeded and chopped
1 can (3 or 4 oz.) sliced mushrooms, drained
1 cup uncooked small shell macaroni
1 cup chicken broth
1 cup cream-style yellow corn
1 cup crushed corn flakes

Melt 2 tablespoons of the butter in a frying pan and in it brown meat on all sides. Sprinkle with salt and pepper. Add celery, green pepper, and mushrooms. Meanwhile, cook macaroni in boiling salted water and drain. Add macaroni to meat mixture, pour over chicken stock, cover, and cook over low heat for 45 minutes.

Turn the macaroni and meat mixture into a 2-quart casserole, spoon over the corn, sprinkle with corn flakes, and dot with the remaining 2 tablespoons butter. Bake, uncovered, in a moderately slow oven (325°) for 50 minutes. Makes 4 to 6 servings.

Mushroom and Veal Ragout (*see suggested menu below*) ✱

1 tablespoon butter
1 pound mushrooms, sliced
1½ pounds boneless veal round steak, cut in bite-size pieces
1½ cups finely diced carrots
½ cup finely diced onion
¼ cup sherry
¼ teaspoon rubbed sage
⅛ teaspoon marjoram
⅛ teaspoon thyme
1½ teaspoons salt
¼ teaspoon pepper
4 egg yolks
3 to 4 tablespoons sour cream
1 package (6 oz.) egg noodles, cooked and drained
Chopped parsley

Melt butter in a heavy frying pan. Add mushrooms; cover and simmer slowly, stirring occasionally, until mushrooms are cooked and there is a quantity of liquid (about 10 minutes). In a 2½-quart casserole combine mushrooms with veal, carrots, onion, sherry, sage, marjoram, thyme, salt, and pepper. Cover and bake in a moderately slow oven (325°) for 1¼ hours.

Drain off juices into a saucepan. Bring to a boil, reduce heat, blend some of the liquid with egg yolks beaten with the sour cream, and stir back into pan. Pour sauce over meat. Add noodles; mix lightly. Sprinkle with chopped parsley. Makes 6 to 8 servings.

✱ *A Company Buffet*

Instant Borsch
Minced Chives   Sour Cream
Mushroom and Veal Ragout with Noodles
(*see recipe above*)
Mixed Green Salad
Bagels or Hard Dinner Rolls
Pineapple Spears   Pear Wedges
Provolone Strips   Freshly Grated Parmesan
Unsalted Crackers

This company meal features borsch, made from a judicious selection of canned foods, and a hearty veal ragout that cooks untended in the oven. For dessert, bring forth a tray of pineapple spears to nibble with thin slices of Provolone cheese, and pear wedges (brushed with lemon juice) to dunk in a bowl of freshly grated Parmesan cheese.

Instant Borsch

1 jar (1 lb.) red cabbage
1 can (1 lb.) shoestring beets and liquid
1 can (15 oz.) French-style onion soup
1 can (10½ oz.) beef bouillon
3 tablespoons red wine vinegar
3 tablespoons brown sugar

In a large pan, combine red cabbage, beets and liquid, onion soup, beef bouillon, wine vinegar, and brown sugar. Bring to a boil and simmer for about 5 minutes (or longer). Serve in bowls and offer a choice of toppings: minced chives or commercial sour cream. Makes 6 to 8 servings.

Veal with Mushrooms and Peppers

Crisply-cooked onion rings top this company veal dish. It cooks in a savory sauce spiced with nutmeg. There will be ample gravy to spoon over steamed, quick-cooking brown rice or cracked wheat.

1½ pounds veal steak
¼ cup salad oil
¼ cup lemon juice
1 teaspoon salt
1 teaspoon paprika
1 clove garlic, minced or mashed
1 teaspoon prepared mustard
¼ teaspoon nutmeg
¼ cup flour
3 tablespoons butter or margarine
1⅓ cups chicken broth
1 green pepper, seeded and cut in strips
¼ pound fresh mushrooms, sliced
1 medium-sized onion, thinly sliced

Marinate meat for at least 15 minutes in a mixture of the oil, lemon juice, salt, paprika, garlic, mustard, and nutmeg. Remove meat from marinade, dredge in flour, and brown on all sides in butter. Mix together the remaining marinade, broth, green pepper, and mushrooms; pour over browned meat. Spoon into a 2-quart casserole. Cover and bake in a moderate oven (350°) for 30 minutes. Remove cover, top with sliced onion rings, and continue baking for 15 minutes longer. Makes 4 generous servings.

Lamb-Stuffed Eggplant Wedges

This method of stuffing eggplant wedges instead of halves is easier, and makes attractive individual servings.

1 large eggplant, cut lengthwise in 4 wedges
Salt
About 3 tablespoons butter or margarine
¾ pound ground lamb
1 small onion, chopped
5 tablespoons finely chopped green pepper
2 tablespoons minced parsley
½ teaspoon salt
¼ teaspoon garlic salt
1 can (8 oz.) tomato sauce
Thin tomato and onion wedges

Sprinkle eggplant with salt. Let stand for about 1 hour, then wipe wedges dry. Melt butter in frying pan and lightly brown cut surface of eggplant wedges. Place them skin side down on a baking sheet and bake in a hot oven (400°) for 10 minutes.

Meanwhile make filling: Add to pan with butter the lamb, chopped onion, 4 tablespoons of the green pepper, parsley, salt, and garlic salt. Cook, stirring, until lightly browned. Split eggplant sections from end to end to make a pocket, running knife down through apex of the wedge. Press pocket open with a spoon and fill with meat mixture, pressing in firmly. Pour tomato sauce into a shallow casserole (about 9 inches square). Set filled eggplant wedges, skin side down, into sauce. Top each wedge with alternating slices of tomato and onion, sprinkle with remaining chopped green pepper. Bake, uncovered, in a moderately hot oven (375°) for 30 minutes. Makes 4 servings.

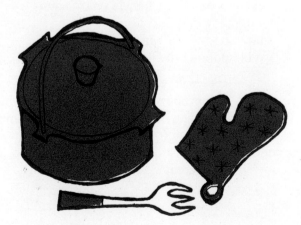

Mousaka Dubrovnik

This meat and eggplant casserole came from a chef in the town of Dubrovnik, Yugoslavia. The dish is made in three steps, any or all of which can be done ahead. Reheat any leftovers in a warm oven (200°) for about 20 to 30 minutes.

Meat filling:
3 large onions, finely chopped
1 clove garlic, minced
¼ cup (⅛ lb.) butter or margarine
1 pound lean lamb, ground with ½ pound
    each lean pork and beef
2 whole eggs
½ teaspoon salt
¼ teaspoon pepper
¼ cup soft bread crumbs

Eggplant mixture:
3 medium-sized eggplants, peeled and cut
    in ¼-inch-thick slices lengthwise
Salt
Flour
5 whole eggs, beaten
Salad oil, butter, or margarine
    (about ⅔ cup)

Sauce crust:
¼ cup (⅛ lb.) butter or margarine
6 tablespoons flour
2 cups milk
½ teaspoon salt
⅛ teaspoon nutmeg
3 egg yolks, beaten

In a large frying pan, simmer onions and garlic in butter until transparent. Mix together ground meat, eggs, salt, pepper, and bread crumbs. Add to onions; stir and cook over medium heat until meat is crumbled and lightly browned.

Sprinkle eggplant slices with salt and let drain for about 15 minutes. Dust slices with flour, dip in egg, and brown a few slices at a time in hot oil or butter (about 350° in an electric frying pan). The eggplant will be just partially cooked at this stage. Line a shallow 3½ or 4-quart casserole with a layer of eggplant, then a layer of the meat mixture. Repeat layers until you have used all the eggplant and meat, ending with a top layer of eggplant.

In a small pan melt butter for sauce and blend in flour. Stir in milk, salt, and nutmeg. Cook, stirring constantly, until thickened. Mix a little of the hot mixture into egg yolks and beat back into sauce. Pour evenly over the top of eggplant. Bake, uncovered, in a moderately hot oven (375° for 1 hour. (If you want to keep the casserole hot for several hours, reduce oven temperature as low as possible—200° or less.)

Cut into squares and top each serving with a dollop of sour cream. Makes 8 to 10 servings.

Lamb Chop Casserole

Eggplant, corn, and shoulder lamb chops go together to make this a flavorful one-dish meal.

4 shoulder lamb chops
About 3 tablespoons salad oil
1 medium-sized eggplant, peeled and
    cut in ¼-inch slices
¼ cup evaporated milk
15 cheese-flavored crackers, crushed
1 can (12 oz.) whole kernel corn
1 can (8 oz.) tomato sauce
¼ teaspoon garlic salt
¼ teaspoon freshly ground pepper
½ teaspoon salt
½ teaspoon dried parsley flakes

In a frying pan, sauté chops in oil until browned on both sides. Remove from the pan. Dip eggplant in milk, then in cracker crumbs; sauté in the drippings (add more oil if necessary), turning once to brown both sides. In a greased 2-quart casserole, alternate layers of corn and eggplant slices; top with browned chops; pour over tomato sauce seasoned with garlic salt, pepper, salt, and parsley flakes. Cover and bake in a moderate oven (350°) for 1 hour or until meat is tender. Makes 4 servings.

Lamb Shank Oven Stew *(see suggested menu below)* ✱

4 lamb shanks, cracked
2 tomatoes, peeled and quartered, or
  1 cup stewed tomatoes
2 cups water
2 teaspoons salt
2 teaspoons paprika
6 to 8 carrots, peeled and cut in half
Flour
Water

Place lamb shanks in a large casserole. Add tomatoes. Pour water over lamb. Sprinkle with salt and paprika. Bake, uncovered, in a moderately hot oven (375°) for 30 minutes. Turn shanks over and bake for 30 minutes more. Add carrots. Bake, covered, at 375° for 30 minutes longer, or until meat is tender. Remove lamb shanks and carrots to warm serving platter. Skim excess fat from cooking juices in casserole. Heat juices over direct heat and thicken with a flour and water paste. Serve over rice or cracked wheat. Makes 4 servings.

✱ November Family Dinner

Lamb Shank Oven Stew *(see recipe above)*
Rice or Cracked Wheat   Meat-Tomato Gravy
Minted Tossed Green Salad
Melba Toast Strips
Fresh Winter Pears

Meaty lamb shanks simmered in a flavorful and colorful oven stew are an ideal main course for a family dinner on a cool November day. Accompany the meat and vegetables with rice or cracked wheat topped with gravy made of thickened meat juices.

Minted Green Salad

Mix broken, crisp salad greens with finely sliced green onions and a dressing of mint vinegar (or white wine vinegar and dried mint flakes), oil, and freshly ground black pepper.

Lamb Eggplant Lebanese

A popular Arab-world combination, lamb and eggplant, is the basis of this casserole.

1½ pounds lean lamb, cut in ½-inch cubes
1 large onion, coarsely chopped
2 small tomatoes, peeled, diced, and drained
⅓ cup pine nuts or sliced almonds
1 teaspoon monosodium glutamate
½ teaspoon pepper
⅛ teaspoon cinnamon
2 teaspoons salt
1 medium-sized eggplant, peeled and cut
  into ¾-inch slices
Butter
1 can (8 oz.) tomato sauce

Mix together lamb cubes, onion, tomatoes, pine nuts, monosodium glutamate, pepper, cinnamon, and 1 teaspoon of the salt. Spoon this mixture into a buttered 2-quart casserole. Lightly brown eggplant on both sides in butter, then arrange over the meat mixture.

Season tomato sauce with remaining 1 teaspoon salt, and pour it over eggplant slices. Bake, uncovered, in a moderately slow oven (325°) for 2 hours. Makes 4 servings.

Yugoslavian casserole "Juvedge" has layers of pork chops, vegetables, rice, and lamb chops.

Juvedge

The vegetable quantities in this Yugoslavian casserole are ample for 6 hearty servings. Vary the number of chops to suit your preference.

3 medium-sized onions, sliced
3 medium-sized tomatoes, sliced
2 large potatoes, peeled and sliced
2 medium-sized green peppers, seeded
 and cut into thin rings
3 to 6 lamb chops
3 to 6 pork chops
1 to 2 tablespoons salad oil
½ cup uncooked regular rice
3 teaspoons salt
Dash pepper
1 teaspoon thyme
1 teaspoon sweet basil
½ cup shredded Cheddar cheese

Arrange a third of the sliced vegetables in a large (5 to 6-quart) casserole. Brown the lamb and pork chops in oil, turning once. Place the lamb chops over the vegetables in the dish; sprinkle with about a third of the seasonings. Add another third of the vegetables and the pork chops. Sprinkle

rice and another third of the seasonings over the chops. Top with remaining vegetables and seasonings. Cover; cook in a moderate oven (350°) for 1½ hours, or until meat is tender. Sprinkle cheese over the vegetables; return to the oven for 5 minutes, uncovered. Makes 6 servings.

Lamb Parmesan

This braised lamb casserole dish has unusual character. Serve it over steamed rice, pilaff, or wild rice.

1 boned leg of lamb (about 5 pounds)
⅓ cup flour
⅓ cup olive oil
2 cloves garlic, crushed
1 can (10½ oz.) mushroom soup
1 can (8 oz.) tomato sauce
2 cups Marsala wine
2 tablespoons sour cream
1 onion, thinly sliced
1 cup fresh mushrooms (whole)
1 tablespoon chicken stock base or 2 bouillon
 cubes
2 teaspoons salt
¾ teaspoon pepper
½ teaspoon marjoram
Parmesan cheese

Cut meat into ¼-inch slices, trimming off fat as you go. Lightly dip in flour, then brown in olive oil heated with 1 clove of the garlic. Place in a 3-quart casserole. In another pan or bowl, combine all remaining ingredients except Parmesan cheese. Blend well and pour over lamb. Sprinkle with Parmesan cheese and bake, uncovered, in a moderate oven (350°) for 1 hour, stirring twice. Makes 6 to 8 servings.

Lamb Pot Pie

The pleasantly light character of this lamb pie is due in part to lemon used discreetly, as well as to the chicken stock base and the parsley potato topping.

2 pounds lamb shoulder, cut in 1-inch squares
Flour
4 tablespoons salad oil
1 cup chicken stock (canned or made from chicken stock base)
10 whole black peppers
1¼ teaspoons salt
1 bay leaf
2 or 3 parsley sprigs, chopped
½ lemon, seeded and thinly sliced
2 large onions, coarsely chopped
2 medium-sized carrots, sliced
2 medium-sized zucchini, sliced
Potato crust (below)

Dust cubes of meat in flour and in a large frying pan, brown on all sides in oil. Add chicken stock, whole peppers, salt, bay leaf, parsley, lemon, and onion; cover and simmer gently for 1½ hours. Add carrots and cook for 15 minutes more; add zucchini and cook for an additional 15 minutes. Turn into a deep 2½ to 3-quart casserole. Spoon potato crust mixture around edges, or decorate with potatoes forced through a large pastry bag with rosette tip. Bake, uncovered, in a very hot oven (425°) for 15 minutes. Makes 6 servings.

Potato crust:
Beat together 3 cups hot mashed potatoes, 4 tablespoons butter, ½ cup minced parsley, and 2 eggs; season to taste with salt and pepper.

In Lamb Pot Pie, parsley-flecked mashed potatoes encircle chunks of lamb, carrots, and zucchini in a steaming lemon-flavored chicken base.

Double Rice and Meat Casserole

The nut-like flavor of wild rice predominates in this casserole.

1 pound fresh mushrooms, sliced
1 small onion, finely chopped
½ pound lean pork, cut in 1-inch cubes
½ pound veal, cut in 1-inch cubes
¼ cup (⅛ lb.) butter or margarine
½ cup uncooked wild rice
½ cup uncooked white rice
4 tablespoons (¼ cup) soy sauce
2 cups sliced celery
1 can (10½ oz.) mushroom soup
½ cup water

Sauté mushrooms, onion, and meat cubes in butter until meat is well browned; turn mixture into a 3-quart casserole. Wash wild rice well and add to meat mixture along with white rice. Add the soy sauce, celery, mushroom soup, and water; mix well. Cover and bake in a moderately slow oven (325°) for 1 hour and 45 minutes. Makes 8 servings.

Chinese Medley

This casserole with many crunchy textures is also very tender, light, and airy. You might put soy sauce on the table when you serve it.

1 pound lean pork steak, cut in ½-inch cubes
Seasoned flour (½ cup flour, 1 teaspoon salt, ¼ teaspoon pepper, ½ teaspoon paprika)
1 tablespoon shortening or salad oil
1 tablespoon grated fresh ginger or preserved ginger
2 cups chopped celery
1 cup chopped onion
¼ cup chopped green pepper
4 to 5 ounces Oriental noodles, or any fine spaghetti
Boiling salted water
1 can (10½ oz.) mushroom soup
1 can (3 or 4 oz.) sliced mushrooms
1 teaspoon monosodium glutamate
½ cup soft bread crumbs, mixed with 2 tablespoons melted butter
¼ cup slivered almonds

Toss pork pieces in a paper bag with the seasoned flour. Brown on all sides in the fat. Add ginger, celery, onion, and green pepper; cover and cook over low heat about 15 minutes. Meanwhile, cook the noodles in boiling salted water until they are just tender; drain. Arrange half the noodles in the bottom of a greased casserole (about 1½-quart size).

To the meat and vegetable mixture, add mushroom soup, mushrooms (include mushroom liquid), monosodium glutamate; mix well. Spoon half over noodles in casserole. Repeat with second layers of noodles and meat mixture. Top with buttered crumbs and slivered almonds. Bake, uncovered, in a moderate oven (350°) for about 45 minutes. Makes about 4 servings.

Potato-Topped Pork Pie

You combine leftover pork roast with apple slices and spicy gravy for this casserole. Top with sweet potato and walnuts.

3 cups cut-up leftover pork roast (in approximately 1-inch cubes)
2 tart apples, peeled, cored, and thinly sliced
4 tablespoons brown sugar
¼ teaspoon cinnamon
1 cup leftover pork gravy
3 cups hot mashed sweet potatoes
3 tablespoons butter or margarine
¼ cup light cream
1 teaspoon salt
Dash of pepper
½ cup finely chopped walnut meats

In a greased 8-inch square baking pan, alternate layers of the meat, sliced apples, and a mixture of the brown sugar and cinnamon. Pour over the gravy. Beat together until blended the mashed potatoes, butter, cream, salt, and pepper; pile over the meat mixture, spreading evenly. Sprinkle with nut meats. Bake, uncovered, in a moderate oven (350°) for 45 minutes. Makes 6 servings.

Wild Rice-Pork Chop Bake

Here is a rich, flavor-packed, and colorful dish that is prepared with very little effort.

¾ cup wild rice
1 can (10½ oz.) onion soup, undiluted
¼ cup dry white wine or apple cider
4 pork chops, cut 1 inch thick
1 small tart apple, cored
1 medium-sized tomato, sliced
Salt to taste
4 pimiento-stuffed green olives (optional)

Wash rice thoroughly in cold water; drain and turn into a 2-quart casserole. Pour in soup and wine. Arrange chops over the top and sprinkle with salt. Cover and bake in a moderately slow oven (325°) for 1 hour. Uncover and arrange a crosswise slice of apple and a slice of tomato on each chop. Sprinkle lightly with salt. Continue baking, uncovered, for 30 minutes longer. Top each serving with a stuffed olive. Makes 4 servings.

Pork Chop-Lima Bean Scallop

Tomato soup slightly sweetens this pork and bean one-dish meal.

6 pork chops, cut 1 inch thick
1 tablespoon salad oil
1 large onion, sliced
1 can (10¾ oz.) tomato soup
4 cups cooked large dried lima beans
Salt and pepper to taste
1 apple

Brown chops on both sides in the oil; remove from pan. Sauté onion in the drippings until golden brown. Stir in soup and lima beans; cook, stirring until well mixed. Turn beans into a 3-quart casserole. Arrange the chops on top. Sprinkle with salt and pepper to taste. Cut apple in half, core, then slice thinly and arrange apple slices on top of each chop. Cover and bake in a moderately hot oven (375°) for 40 minutes, or until the chops are tender. Makes 6 servings.

Oven-Barbecued Pork Chops

You might want to tuck vegetables such as peeled carrots or thick slices of sweet potatoes between these chops to bake along with them.

4 loin pork chops, cut 1½ inches thick
Salt and pepper
4 slices lemon, ¼ inch thick
4 center slices from a large onion,
    ¼ inch thick
½ cup brown sugar, firmly packed
¾ cup catsup

Brown chops in a frying pan, arrange in a 9-inch square baking dish or casserole, and season with salt and pepper. Top each chop with a slice of lemon and a slice of onion. Mix together brown sugar and catsup and pour over the meat—be sure the top of each piece is coated with sauce. Cover and bake in a moderately slow oven (325°) for 1 hour, basting occasionally. Remove cover and bake for an additional 30 minutes, basting frequently. Makes 4 servings.

Cornbread and raisin dressing bake with browned pork chops. Green beans are good accompaniment.

Pork Chops with Cornbread and Raisin Dressing

Browned pork chops are placed over cornbread dressing before you bake this dish. The cornbread for the dressing can be made from a mix the day before.

4 loin or rib pork chops
2 teaspoons salt
¾ teaspoon pepper
1 small onion, chopped
½ cup chopped celery
2 cups day-old cornbread crumbs
1½ cups day-old bread cubes
¾ cup raisins
⅓ cup milk

Trim all but a thin layer of fat from chops. In a frying pan render some of the fat to coat pan lightly; discard excess fat. Rub 1½ teaspoons of the salt and ½ teaspoon of the pepper into pork. Sauté pork over medium heat until browned on both sides. Remove from pan and set aside.

In the same pan, sauté the onion and celery. Add remaining ½ teaspoon salt and ¼ teaspoon pepper. Mix the onion and celery with the cornbread, bread cubes, and raisins. Stir in milk. Spread bread mixture in the bottom of a greased 1½-quart casserole. Place chops over dressing and bake in a moderate oven (350°) for about 1 hour, or until tender. Makes 4 servings.

Ham and Chicken Pie *(see suggested menu below)* ✱

You combine cooked meats with canned soup and seasonings, and then top this casserole with refrigerator biscuits.

1 can (10½ oz.) cream of mushroom soup
½ cup milk
⅛ teaspoon marjoram
⅛ teaspoon thyme
¼ cup chopped onion
½ cup finely chopped celery
1 cup diced cooked ham
1 cup diced cooked chicken or turkey
1 cup cooked green peas
1 package (8 oz.) refrigerator biscuits
Melted butter
2 tablespoons poppy seed

Combine cream of mushroom soup with milk, marjoram, thyme, onion, and celery. Pour half this mixture into a buttered shallow casserole (1½-quart size). Top mixture with ham, chicken or turkey, and peas. Pour over remaining soup mixture.

Arrange biscuits on top. Brush biscuits with melted butter and sprinkle with poppy seed. Bake in a moderate oven (350°) for about 30 minutes, or until mixture bubbles and biscuits are brown. Makes 4 servings.

✱ One-Dish Sunday Supper

Ham and Chicken Pie with Biscuit Topping
(see recipe above)
Carrot Curls   Raw Turnip Sticks
Hot Minted Fruit Cocktail   Vanilla Wafers

For a quick Sunday supper, here's a dish that combines cooked ham and leftover chicken or turkey. Along with the Ham and Chicken Pie, serve raw vegetables and a simple fruit cocktail dessert.

Hot Minted Fruit Cocktail

Heat 1 can (1 lb.) fruit cocktail to simmering with ¼ teaspoon finely chopped mint. Stir in 1 cup chopped fresh apple, remove from heat, and serve. Makes 4 servings.

Pork Chops and Sweet Potatoes

Pork chops are layered with sweet potatoes, apples, and raisins for this dish.

4 loin or rib pork chops
1 teaspoon salt
¼ teaspoon pepper
1 tablespoon flour
1 cup water
¾ cup raisins
1 tablespoon lemon juice
2 apples, peeled and quartered
2 sweet potatoes, peeled and quartered

Trim fat from chops; render some in frying pan to coat lightly; discard excess fat. Rub meat with salt and pepper. Sauté pork until browned on both sides. Remove chops from pan. In the same pan, add flour and mix until blended. Gradually stir in water, raisins, and lemon juice. Simmer 5 minutes. Layer half of the apples and potatoes in a greased 2-quart casserole. Place chops on top. Layer remaining apples and potatoes over chops and pour sauce over all. Cover and bake in a moderate oven (350°) for 1 hour, or until meat is tender. Makes 4 servings.

Ham-Macaroni Casserole

This ham and macaroni combination, of German origin, bears little resemblance to the usual macaroni casserole. It is very meaty, has a crusty top, and is served with a tomato mushroom sauce.

1¼ cups elbow macaroni
Boiling, salted water
¼ cup (⅛ lb.) butter or margarine
2 eggs, separated
1½ cups coarsely chopped cooked ham
2 tablespoons grated Parmesan cheese
1 can (8 oz.) tomato sauce
¼ cup water
1 tablespoon lemon juice
1½ teaspoons sliced green onion tops or chives
1 can (3 to 4 oz.) mushroom slices, drained

Cook the macaroni in boiling, salted water about 15 minutes; drain and cool. Cream butter, add the egg yolks and the ham; mix together and mix thoroughly with the cooked macaroni.

Beat the egg whites until they form stiff peaks; then quickly mix them in with the macaroni mixture. Turn into a buttered 2-quart casserole; sprinkle top with the cheese. Bake, uncovered, in a moderately hot oven (375°) for about 45 minutes or until nicely browned on top.

Make tomato-mushroom sauce by combining the canned tomato sauce, water, lemon juice, green onions, and mushrooms in a small pan; heat through. Serve warm to spoon over the casserole. Makes 4 servings.

Tamale Ham Pie

Ham, raisins, and a topping of corn muffin mix create a savory variation of the classic tamale pie.

1 large onion, chopped
½ small green pepper, chopped
2 tablespoons salad or olive oil
1 tablespoon flour
1 clove garlic, minced or mashed
2 cups diced cooked ham
1 can (12 oz.) whole kernel corn
2¼ cups tomato juice
¼ cup seedless raisins
1 teaspoon chili powder
1 package (8 oz.) corn muffin mix

Using a large frying pan, sauté onion and green pepper in oil until onion is golden brown. Blend in flour. Stir in garlic, ham, corn, tomato juice, raisins, and chili powder; heat to boiling.

While ham mixture heats, prepare muffin mix as directed on package. Pour hot ham mixture into a greased 8 by 12-inch baking dish; spoon corn muffin batter around edges. Bake in a moderately hot oven (375°) for 25 minutes, or until topping is golden brown. Makes 6 to 8 servings.

Ham-stuffed Peppers

Ham, onions, and three kinds of cheese—what more could a green pepper want? For big party spreads, this dish is a high-flavored accompaniment for buffet roasts and cold chicken. For family meals, it's a hearty main dish.

5 large green peppers
Boiling salted water
2 cups diced ham
4 slices dry French bread, crumbled
¾ cup shredded sharp Cheddar cheese
½ cup shredded jack cheese
6 green onions with tops, finely chopped
1 egg, beaten
5 slices jack cheese

Slice off the stem ends of peppers; remove seeds and veins. Parboil for 5 minutes in the boiling salted water; drain. Mix together ham, bread crumbs, Cheddar and shredded jack cheese, onions, and the beaten egg. Spoon the ham and cheese mixture into peppers. Top each with a slice of the jack cheese. Place in a greased shallow pan (about 9 inches square) and bake, uncovered, in a moderately hot oven (375°) for about 20 minutes, or until peppers are tender and the cheese bubbly. Makes 5 servings.

Ham Potato Scallop

Cheese sauce, celery, and flecks of green pepper are added to scalloped potatoes and ham in this flavorful and mellow casserole.

1 medium-sized onion, finely chopped
3 tablespoons butter or margarine
3 tablespoons flour
1 teaspoon salt
⅛ teaspoon pepper
½ teaspoon dry mustard
1½ cups milk
¾ cup shredded sharp Cheddar cheese
4 medium-sized potatoes, sliced ¼ inch thick
1½ cups diced, cooked ham
½ cup sliced celery
½ cup finely chopped green pepper

Sauté onion in melted butter until tender. Stir in flour, salt, pepper, and mustard. Gradually pour in milk, and stirring constantly, cook until sauce is thickened. Add cheese and stir until blended. In a greased 2½-quart casserole, alternate layers of sliced raw potato, diced ham, sliced celery, and chopped green pepper; pour over part of the cheese sauce, and continue to arrange ingredients in layers until all are used. Pour remaining cheese sauce over all. Bake, covered, in a moderate oven (350°) for 1 hour; remove cover and continue baking 30 minutes longer, or until potatoes are tender and lightly browned on top. Makes 8 servings.

Wild Rice and Ham Casserole

This wild rice and sliced ham casserole owes part of its elegance to the creamy sherry-flavored sauce that goes all through it.

2 cups wild rice or brown rice
Boiling salted water
1 large can (6 or 8 oz.) sliced mushrooms
2 cups milk
2 tablespoons cornstarch
2 tablespoons water
¼ cup sherry
1 teaspoon soy sauce
Salt and pepper to taste
8 slices cooked ham, cut in half
1 can (about 1 lb.) artichoke hearts
¼ pound (1 cup) shredded Cheddar cheese

Cook wild rice in boiling salted water until just tender but not mushy. Drain liquid from mushrooms into a saucepan. Add the milk and heat until scalding. Mix cornstarch with water to make a paste, and stir in. Stirring constantly, cook until thickened. Stir in sherry, soy sauce, and salt and pepper to taste, remembering that ham will add some saltiness.

In a greased 3-quart casserole, arrange layers of rice, ham, mushrooms, and halved artichoke hearts; then repeat the layers. Pour over the sherry-flavored cream sauce and sprinkle with shredded cheese. Bake, uncovered, in a slow oven (300°) for 1 hour, or until it is thoroughly heated. Makes 6 to 8 servings.

Italian Baked Liver with Mushroom-Olive Sauce

This method of preparing liver is unusual in that you don't brown it; just pour the sauce over it and bake.

2 pounds sliced beef liver
1 medium-sized onion, chopped
1 clove garlic, minced or mashed
1 tablespoon flour
½ cup catsup
1 teaspoon minced parsley
½ cup chopped celery
½ cup chopped green pepper
1 can (4 oz.) mushroom stems and pieces
1 small can (about 4 oz.) pitted ripe olives
2 tablespoons olive oil or salad oil
1 can (8 oz.) tomato sauce
1 cup water
1 teaspoon oregano
1 teaspoon salt
½ teaspoon pepper

Place liver slices in a greased baking pan or dish (about 9 by 13-inch size). Combine onion, garlic, flour, catsup, parsley, celery, green pepper, mushrooms, ripe olives, olive oil, tomato sauce, water, oregano, salt, and pepper; mix until well blended, and pour mixture over liver. Bake uncovered, in a moderate oven (350°) for 30 to 40 minutes, or until tender. Makes 6 to 8 servings.

Chicken Liver Casserole

Colorful pimientos and olives, crisp celery, and flavorful mushrooms dress up fried chicken livers. Steamed rice is an excellent side dish.

5 tablespoons butter or margarine
½ pound chicken livers or
   1 package (8 oz.) frozen chicken livers
2 stalks celery, thinly sliced
¼ cup flour
1½ cups milk
¾ teaspoon salt
⅛ teaspoon pepper
2 canned pimientos, cut in thin strips
6 ripe olives, sliced
1 small can (3 or 4 oz.) sliced mushrooms, drained

Melt butter in frying pan, and fry chicken livers in it until browned; remove. Add sliced celery to drippings and cook for 5 minutes. Stir in flour, then add milk gradually to make a sauce. Season with salt and pepper, and add pimientos and olives. Arrange layers of the fried livers, sauce, and mushrooms in a greased 1-quart casserole. Cover and bake in a moderately hot oven (375°) for 20 minutes. Makes 4 servings.

Potato and Sausage Bake

Sausage doubles as an herb seasoning and a meat in this one-dish meal. You can draw from your staples for the ingredients.

3 medium-sized potatoes, peeled and
   cut in quarters
½ pound bulk pork sausage
1 medium-sized onion, finely chopped
1 cup cubed day-old bread
1 egg, slightly beaten
½ cup milk
½ cup water
½ teaspoon salt
¼ teaspoon pepper

Peel potatoes, cut in quarters, and cook in boiling salted water until tender; drain and dice potatoes. Meanwhile, brown crumbled sausage in a frying pan with the chopped onion until onion is golden brown. Stir in the bread cubes. Combine egg and milk and pour into the pan with the browned meat and onion. Add water, salt, and pepper. Combine with the diced potatoes and turn into a greased 1½-quart casserole. Cover and bake in a moderate oven (350°) for 30 minutes or until the liquid is absorbed. Remove cover during the last few minutes of baking to brown the top. Makes 4 servings.

Frankfurter Casserole

As this casserole bakes, some of the seasoning in the frankfurters goes down into the rice, spinach, and cheese.

2 packages (10 oz. each) frozen chopped spinach
2 cups cooked rice (¾ cup quick-cooking rice)
8 slices bacon
⅔ cup shredded American cheese
1 pound frankfurters
½ cup liquid from cooking spinach
1 tablespoon Worcestershire
1 teaspoon garlic salt

Cook spinach as directed on the package; drain, reserving liquid. Place alternate layers of spinach and rice in a well-buttered 2-quart casserole. Partially cook bacon and drain on paper towels. Sprinkle the cheese over the top of the rice and spinach; arrange frankfurters over the cheese. Mix together the ½ cup liquid from cooking spinach, Worcestershire, and garlic salt; pour over frankfurters. Arrange bacon over the frankfurters. Bake, uncovered, in a moderately slow oven (325°) for 45 minutes. Makes 8 servings.

Wiener Mix-Up

Quickly prepared, colorful, well seasoned, inexpensive—all are true of this casserole dish.

1 pound frankfurters, thinly sliced
1 can (4½ oz.) chopped ripe olives
1 can (1 lb.) whole kernel corn, drained
1 can (1 lb.) cut green beans, drained
1 cup (¼ lb.) diced Cheddar cheese
2 cups tomato catsup
1 tablespoon sugar
½ teaspoon salt
⅛ teaspoon garlic salt
1 small onion, finely chopped

Mix sliced frankfurters with olives, whole kernel corn, green beans, cheese, catsup, sugar, salt, garlic salt, and chopped onion. Turn into lightly greased 2½-quart casserole. Cover and bake in a moderate oven (350°) for 1 hour. Makes 6 to 8 servings.

Beef Heart with Green Noodles

Firm-textured heart muscle will be tender when cooked slowly with moist heat. You remove the fat and cut away the tubes for best flavor. Heart takes especially well to creamy sauces, as in this casserole.

1 beef heart (3 to 3½ lbs.)
Water
1 teaspoon salt
2 carrots
1 onion
1 bay leaf
5 or 6 whole black peppers
3 cups green noodles, cooked and drained
½ teaspoon caraway seed
1 can (10½ oz.) cream of mushroom soup
1 soup can milk
3 slices American cheese
½ cup toasted rye bread crumbs, mixed
    with 2 tablespoons melted butter
6 fresh mushrooms, sliced

Cut away tough membrane, tubes, and fat from top and inside heart. Wash in clear water. Place in a kettle and cover with water; add salt, carrots, onion, bay leaf, and peppers. Bring to a boil, cover, and simmer slowly for about 2½ hours or until heart is tender. (Or you can cook heart in a pressure saucepan for 1 hour at pressure indicated for meats.) Slice heart; save stock for soups. Alternate layers of heart and noodles in a casserole (about 3-quart size), sprinkling each layer with caraway seed. Dilute mushroom soup with milk and pour over heart and noodles. Top with cheese, sprinkle with crumbs, and decorate with mushrooms. Bake, uncovered, in a moderately slow oven (325°) for 20 minutes, or until heated through. Makes 8 servings.

Poultry Casseroles

Party casseroles, family favorites

Cheddar Chicken Casserole

Chunks of chicken and crunchy cashews turn this macaroni and cheese casserole into company fare. It's a good choice for a potluck supper.

1 package (1 lb.) frozen chicken breasts
2 cups water
3 green onions, cut in pieces
3 celery tops
1 cup elbow macaroni
¼ pound (1 cup) shredded Cheddar cheese
½ cup cashew nut meats
2 cans (10½ oz.) cream of chicken soup
¾ cup crushed Cheddar cheese crackers

Simmer chicken breasts in water with onions and celery tops until tender, about 25 minutes. Strain off broth and reserve. Let chicken cool slightly, then skin; remove meat from bones, and break into chunks. Meanwhile, cook macaroni in boiling salted water until almost tender; drain and turn into a greased 2-quart casserole. Sprinkle shredded cheese over macaroni, cover with chicken. Sprinkle with nut meats and pour over the soup, thinned with ⅔ cup of the reserved chicken stock. Top with crackers and bake, uncovered, in a moderate oven (350°) for 30 minutes, until bubbly. If this dish is prepared ahead and refrigerated, bake it for 45 minutes at 350°. Makes 6 servings.

Chicken with Ginger

Chicken, mushrooms, and green beans are mixed in this company casserole.

2 whole chicken breasts, split
4 thighs
6 tablespoons butter or margarine
½ pound mushrooms, sliced
⅔ cup flour
2 teaspoons salt
1 teaspoon sage
1 teaspoon thyme
¼ teaspoon pepper
1 lemon, cut in half
1¼ teaspoons shredded fresh ginger or ½ teaspoon ground ginger
2 packages (9 oz. each) cut green beans, thawed

Wash chicken and dry well. Melt 2 tablespoons of the butter in a frying pan. Sauté mushrooms about 5 minutes; remove from pan and reserve. Combine flour with salt, sage, thyme, and pepper. Rub chicken with lemon to moisten; dust lightly with flour mixture. Melt remaining 4 tablespoons butter in the frying pan and brown chicken well; remove to a 2-quart casserole, sprinkle with ginger. Dust green beans with some of the seasoned flour; brown lightly in same pan, adding more butter if needed. Mix beans with mushrooms; spoon over chicken. Bake, covered, in a hot oven (400°) about 40 minutes. Makes 4 to 6 servings.

Chicken Marengo (page 31) is a delicious stew-type entree which combines chicken, fresh tomatoes, mushrooms, and small white onions. Serve a cracked wheat pilaff or rice so none of the flavorful sauce is wasted.

Chicken in Casserole with Grapes

Green grapes and sautéed sliced mushrooms are the finishing touch on this delicately seasoned chicken baked in a light wine sauce. Choose a favorite cracked wheat pilaf as a complement.

2 whole chicken breasts, split
4 thighs
4 drumsticks
Salt and pepper
Flour
5 tablespoons butter or margarine
¼ cup minced onion
¼ cup chicken broth
¾ cup dry white wine
½ pound mushrooms, sliced
3 tablespoons butter or margarine
2 cups seeded Muscat grapes or
    Thompson seedless grapes

Sprinkle chicken with salt and pepper and coat lightly with flour. Heat the 5 tablespoons butter in a frying pan and quickly brown chicken on all sides. Arrange pieces closely together in a single layer in a large shallow baking pan. Add onion to butter in frying pan; cook until soft. Add chicken broth and wine; bring to a boil, then pour over chicken. Bake, covered, in a moderately hot oven (375°) for 40 minutes.

Meanwhile, sauté mushrooms in the 3 tablespoons butter. When chicken has cooked for 40 minutes, add mushrooms and grapes; continue baking, covered, for 8 minutes more, or until grapes are just heated. Arrange on a platter or serve from a chafing dish. Makes 6 to 8 servings.

Chicken Divan

To simplify the preparation of this rather complicated, well known casserole, you might cook the chicken, broccoli, and sauces a day ahead and refrigerate them separately. Just before serving, assemble the casserole and whip and fold the cream into the sauce.

3 packages (1 lb. each) chicken breasts
2 cups water
1 tablespoon salt
Celery leaves
1 medium-sized onion, quartered
2 pounds fresh broccoli, or 2 packages (10 oz. each) frozen broccoli
2 cups medium white sauce (made with half milk and half chicken stock)
½ cup Hollandaise sauce (canned sauce or your own recipe)
¾ teaspoon salt
3 tablespoons sherry
1 teaspoon Worcestershire
1 cup (¼ lb.) grated Parmesan cheese
½ cup whipping cream

Simmer chicken in water with the 1 tablespoon salt, celery leaves, and onion until tender, about 25 minutes. Let cool. Remove skin and bones and slice the chicken meat. Separate broccoli into flowerets, and cook in boiling salted water until tender, about 15 minutes.

Combine the white sauce, Hollandaise sauce, the ¾ teaspoon salt, sherry, and Worcestershire. Butter a large, shallow casserole (about 3-quart size), and arrange broccoli spears, spoke-fashion, around the edge; place the remainder in the center of the dish. Sprinkle with half the grated cheese. Arrange sliced chicken on top. Whip cream and fold into combined sauces; spoon over chicken. Sprinkle with remaining cheese.

Bake, uncovered, in a hot oven (400°) for 20 minutes (be careful not to overcook). Then place about 5 inches under broiler and broil until lightly browned and bubbly. Makes 6 to 8 servings.

Chicken Marengo

After the battle of Marengo, Napoleon's chef is supposed to have created a fine dish from one small hen, 6 crayfish, 4 tomatoes, 3 eggs, a little garlic, and oil. This modern version uses more ingredients, but should please your guests as much as the original dish pleased Napoleon.

16 small white onions, peeled
1 clove garlic, minced or mashed
2 cups small whole, or sliced, fresh mushrooms
¼ cup olive oil or salad oil
2 broiler-fryer chickens (about 3 lbs. each), quartered, including giblets
8 medium-sized tomatoes, peeled and quartered
1 tablespoon salt
¼ teaspoon freshly ground pepper
1 or 2 sprigs parsley
1 celery top
1 carrot, quartered
1 bay leaf
1 sprig fresh thyme or 1 teaspoon dried thyme
2 cups water
¾ cup flour
1 cup dry white wine (or ¼ cup lemon juice and ¾ cup water)

Sauté onions, garlic, and mushrooms in 2 tablespoons of the oil in a large ovenproof frying pan or Dutch oven. Remove onions and mushrooms from pan with a slotted spoon and set aside. Add remaining 2 tablespoons oil to the pan and brown chicken well on all sides. Add tomatoes, onions, mushrooms, salt, and pepper. Cover and bake in a moderate oven (350°) for 1 hour, or until chicken is tender.

Meanwhile, make a bouquet garni by tying together in a piece of cheesecloth the parsley, celery top, carrot, bay leaf, and thyme (use a long string so bouquet can easily be removed from pan). Simmer chicken giblets and neck with bouquet garni in the water about 25 minutes, reserve stock. When chicken is tender, remove it from the pan along with vegetables; place chicken and vegetables in a greased 3-quart casserole; keep warm. Blend flour with wine (or lemon juice and water) until smooth and creamy. Stir into pan drippings. Add 1 cup of the stock from cooked giblets and cook over medium heat, stirring constantly, until sauce is thick and smooth. Pour sauce over chicken in casserole. Serve immediately, or refrigerate. Reheat, covered, in a moderate oven (350°) for about 1 hour just before serving time. Makes 8 generous servings.

Tarragon Chicken Casserole

Just top pieces of chicken with onion, seasonings, and canned soup to make this flavorful entrée.

1 broiler-fryer (2½-3 lbs.), cut in pieces
1 to 2 medium-sized onions, chopped
1½ teaspoons tarragon
¼ teaspoon poultry seasoning
1¼ teaspoons salt
¼ teaspoon pepper
1 can (10½ oz.) cream of chicken soup
¼ cup milk
¼ cup almonds, sliced or slivered (optional)

In a rectangular baking pan (about 13 by 9 inches) arrange chicken, skin side up; do not overlap pieces. Scatter onions over chicken along with tarragon, poultry seasoning, salt, and pepper. Mix cream of chicken soup with milk and spoon over chicken.

Bake, uncovered, in a moderately hot oven (375°) for 40 minutes. Sprinkle chicken with almonds, if desired. Bake 10 minutes more or until chicken is tender. Makes 4 to 6 servings.

Chicken and Artichoke Casserole

You can make this chicken casserole completely in advance and refrigerate it, or, if you prefer, bake and serve it at once. It is quite filling by itself, but you may want to add a rice dish to your menu for hearty appetites.

1 or 2 sprigs parsley
1 celery top
1 carrot, quartered
1 bay leaf
1 sprig fresh thyme or 1 teaspoon dried thyme
2 broiler-fryers (about 3 lbs. each) cut in pieces
1 tablespoon salt
¼ teaspoon freshly ground pepper
2 cups water
2 packages (10 oz. each) frozen artichoke hearts, thawed
¼ cup butter or margarine
¼ cup flour
3 cups shredded mild Cheddar cheese
½ teaspoon nutmeg
½ cup fine dry bread crumbs
1 teaspoon savory
1 teaspoon thyme,
2 tablespoons butter or margarine

Make a bouquet garni by tying together in a piece of cheesecloth the parsley, celery top, carrot, bay leaf, and thyme (use a long string so bouquet can easily be removed from pan). Place chicken pieces, bouquet garni, salt, pepper, and water in a large pan. Cover and simmer about 1 hour, or until chicken is tender. Cool chicken in stock. Then remove meat from bones in good-sized pieces and arrange in 3-quart casserole along with artichoke hearts; reserve stock.

To make cheese sauce, melt butter and blend in flour until smooth. Gradually add 2 cups of the chicken stock. Cook, stirring constantly, until thick and smooth. Then stir in cheese and nutmeg. Pour sauce over chicken and artichoke hearts. Sprinkle with bread crumbs, savory, and thyme; dot with butter. (At this point, you may refrigerate the casserole, covered, until you are ready to heat it for serving.) Bake, uncovered, in a moderate oven (350°) for 30 minutes or until golden brown. Makes 8 servings.

Artichoke hearts and savory chunks of chicken bake in a creamy, herb-flavored cheese sauce.

Baked Almond Chicken

This baked chicken is enriched by an herb butter, almonds, and light cream. Sour cream, added late in the cooking, thickens the sauce.

1 broiler-fryer (about 3½ lbs.) cut in pieces
Flour
1 teaspoon celery salt
1 teaspoon paprika
1 teaspoon salt
½ teaspoon curry powder
½ teaspoon oregano, crushed
½ teaspoon freshly ground pepper
6 tablespoons melted butter or margarine
¾ cup sliced almonds
1½ cups light cream
½ cup sour cream
3 tablespoons fine dry bread crumbs blended with 1 tablespoon melted butter

Coat chicken pieces with flour. Blend celery salt, paprika, salt, curry powder, oregano, and pepper with butter; roll chicken pieces in seasoned butter, coating all sides. Arrange chicken in a single layer in a baking dish (about 9 by 13 inches). Sprinkle evenly with almonds. Pour light cream between pieces. Bake, covered, in a moderate oven (350°) for 45 minutes. Uncover; spoon about ½ cup sauce from pan into sour cream and mix together. Pour evenly over chicken. Sprinkle evenly with bread crumbs. Bake, uncovered, about 15 minutes longer or until chicken is tender. Makes 6 servings.

Chicken Sesame (see suggested menu below) ✳

2 broiler-fryers (2½ to 3 lbs. each), cut in pieces
¼ cup flour
¼ cup sesame seed
1 teaspoon salt
½ teaspoon pepper
¼ cup salad oil
½ cup white wine
½ cup chicken stock

Sauce:
1 small onion, chopped
3 stalks celery, chopped
1 medium carrot, chopped
Chicken drippings
1 can (3 or 4 oz.) mushroom pieces
1 cup medium white sauce
1 cup (½ pint) sour cream
1 teaspoon tarragon

Coat each piece of chicken with a mixture made with the flour, sesame seed, salt, and pepper. Brown chicken in salad oil; transfer browned pieces to a 4-quart casserole. Pour wine and chicken stock over browned chicken, cover and bake in a moderate oven (350°) for 45 minutes.

Meanwhile prepare sauce: Simmer vegetables for 10 minutes in chicken drippings that remain in frying pan. Add mushroom pieces (including mushroom liquid), white sauce, sour cream, and tarragon. Pour sauce over chicken and bake, uncovered, for an additional 20 minutes. Makes 8 or 9 servings.

✳ Casserole Supper

Chicken Sesame (*see recipe above*)
Mixed Green Salad with Stuffed Olives
French Dressing
Toasted Onion Bread Spears
Blueberry Supreme

Here is another delicious chicken dish to add to your casserole repertoire, along with a choice blueberry dessert you make the day before you serve it.

Toasted Onion Bread Spears

Cut a slender, buffet-style loaf of French bread into quarters lengthwise. Spread the cut edges with softened butter or margarine and sprinkle with instant minced onion or instant toasted onions. Place on an ungreased baking sheet, buttered sides up, and heat in a moderate oven (350°) for 5 or 6 minutes. Cut in 4 or 5-inch lengths and serve hot. Makes 8 to 10 servings.

Blueberry Supreme

1 box (about 8 oz.) vanilla wafers
1 cup sifted powdered sugar
½ cup (¼ lb.) softened butter
2 eggs
1 can (1 lb., 6 oz.) blueberry pie filling
1 cup (½ pint) heavy cream, whipped
½ cup chopped pecans

Crush vanilla wafers and spread half the crumbs on the bottom of a 9-inch square or 8 by 10-inch pan. Cream sugar with butter; add eggs, one at a time, and beat well. Spread egg mixture over vanilla wafer layer. Cover with blueberry pie filling. Spread whipped cream over blueberries; sprinkle chopped pecans on whipped cream, and top with remaining vanilla wafer crumbs. Refrigerate for 24 hours. Serve cold. Makes 9 servings.

Chicken with Herb Dumplings

This is a Sunday dinner version of the old favorite, chicken and dumplings. It's a meal-in-one since you cook the chicken with mushrooms, carrots, and onions.

1 stewing hen (3 to 4 lbs.), cut in quarters
2 teaspoons salt
1 teaspoon pepper
3 tablespoons butter, melted
2 whole cloves
8 to 12 small white onions, peeled
4 carrots, peeled
8 fresh mushrooms, or 1 can (3 or 4 oz.)
   whole mushrooms
1 clove garlic, minced or mashed
¼ teaspoon dry marjoram
¼ teaspoon dry thyme
2 sprigs parsley
1 small bay leaf
¾ cup dry white wine
1 cup (½ pint) sour cream

Dumplings:
1 cup packaged biscuit mix
1 tablespoon chopped parsley
6 tablespoons milk

Wash chicken and pat dry on paper towels. Season with salt and pepper. Brown in butter in Dutch oven, or any heavy roasting pan having a tight-fitting cover.

Stick cloves in one onion. Add vegetables, mushrooms, garlic, and seasonings to chicken. Pour in wine. Cover and bake in moderately hot oven (375°) until chicken is tender, about 1 hour.

Meanwhile, make dumplings. Combine biscuit mix with parsley; stir in milk with fork until well moistened. Heat sour cream and add to chicken. Place over medium heat on top of the range, and when mixture is bubbling, drop dumplings from teaspoon around edge of pan. Simmer for 10 minutes uncovered, then 10 minutes covered. Makes 4 servings.

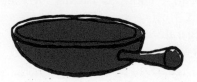

Pineapple Chicken

In this outstanding dish, the pineapple comes through distinctively.

2 packages (1 lb. each) chicken breasts or legs,
   or 1 broiler fryer (approximately 2½ lbs.),
   cut in pieces
¼ cup flour
1½ teaspoons salt
½ teaspoon pepper
¼ teaspoon thyme
5 tablespoons butter or margarine
1 cup (¼ lb.) shredded sharp Cheddar cheese
½ pound cooked ham, cut into strips
1 can (4 oz.) sliced mushrooms
1 can (14 oz.) pineapple tidbits

Roll chicken in flour seasoned with salt, pepper, and thyme. Brown in butter, turning to brown all sides. Transfer to a 2-quart casserole and sprinkle with cheese and ham. Add mushrooms and liquid. Drain pineapple and measure out ¼ cup syrup; add the measured syrup and pineapple tidbits to the casserole. Cover and bake in a moderate oven (350°) for 30 minutes; remove cover and continue baking 10 minutes longer. Makes 4 to 6 servings.

Chicken Pot Pie

Delicately seasoned chunks of chicken fill this pie to capacity. There's just enough creamy sauce to blend meat and vegetables smoothly.

1 stewing hen (4 lbs.), cut in pieces
1 cup white wine (optional)
Water
1 medium-sized onion, cut in fourths
3 stalks celery
1 sprig parsley
1 bay leaf
6 whole black peppers
⅛ teaspoon marjoram
2 teaspoons salt
12 small white onions, peeled
6 small whole carrots
1 package (10 oz.) frozen peas
½ pound small mushrooms
2 tablespoons butter

Chicken for Chicken Pot Pie is stewed in broth flavored with wine and herbs, then combined with vegetables, seasonings, and rich cream sauce and sealed beneath decorated pastry.

2 tablespoons flour
1 tablespoon Worcestershire
1 tablespoon grated lemon peel
2 egg yolks
½ cup light cream
Salt and pepper to taste
Pastry for 1 crust pie
1 whole egg
2 tablespoons light cream

Place chicken in large pan. Add wine and enough water to cover. Add onion, celery, parsley, bay leaf, whole black peppers, marjoram, and salt. Bring to a boil; cover and simmer gently for 2 hours. Let cool. Remove skin and bones of chicken and discard; cut meat in small pieces. Strain and save stock. Cook boiling onions, carrots, and peas separately until each is just barely done, then combine with chicken in a deep, 2½-quart casserole.

Sauté mushrooms in butter for about 5 minutes, sprinkle with flour and blend in 2 cups reserved chicken stock, Worcestershire, and lemon peel. Cook, stirring, until thickened. Beat egg yolks with cream, add to sauce and remove from heat. Season with salt and pepper. Pour sauce over chicken. Cover with pastry, fluting edge and decorating as desired. Cut several slits in crust. Brush with whole egg beaten with the 2 tablespoons cream. Bake in a very hot oven (425°) for 25 minutes. Makes 6 servings.

Chicken and Mushrooms

The addition of fresh mushrooms and wine makes this dish outstanding.

6 tablespoons butter or margarine
¼ teaspoon thyme
1 teaspoon paprika
1 teaspoon salt
¼ teaspoon pepper
1 broiler-fryer (2½ to 3 lbs.), cut in pieces
About ¼ cup flour
½ cup dry white wine
2 cups sliced fresh mushrooms

Melt butter in a baking dish (about 9 by 13 inches) and stir in thyme, paprika, salt, and pepper. Dredge the serving-size pieces of chicken in flour, then swish each around in butter until well coated; arrange them in the baking dish with skin side down. Bake in hot oven (400°) until browned, about 30 minutes. Reduce heat to 350°, turn over chicken pieces, and add the wine. Spread mushrooms over top, cover dish with foil and continue baking about 30 minutes longer, or until tender. To crisp the skin on chicken, set baking dish under broiler for a few minutes. Makes 4 servings.

Sizzling from the broiler come individual casseroles of Chicken Tetrazzini—sauce, noodles, chicken, cheese.

Lemon Chicken

Lemon peel and juice, mint leaves, and chicken are a rather unusual combination in this casserole. A small amount of brown sugar counteracts the acidity of the lemon.

6 to 8 pieces of broiler-fryer (breasts, legs, thighs)
1 whole lemon
⅓ cup flour
1½ teaspoons salt
½ teaspoon paprika
4 tablespoons salad oil or shortening
2 tablespoons brown sugar
1 lemon, thinly sliced
1 cup chicken broth
2 sprigs fresh mint

Wash chicken and drain on paper towels. Grate peel from whole lemon and set aside; cut lemon in half and squeeze juice over pieces of chicken, rubbing each piece with juice. Shake in paper bag with flour, salt, and paprika. Brown chicken slowly in salad oil. Arrange in 2-quart casserole or baking pan.

Sprinkle grated lemon peel over chicken, add brown sugar, and cover with thinly sliced lemon. Pour in broth and place mint over top. Cover and bake in moderately hot oven (375°) until chicken is tender (40 to 45 minutes). Remove mint before serving. Makes 6 to 8 servings.

Chicken Tetrazzini

Luisa Tetrazzini was considered the greatest coloratura soprano of her time, but the reason most of us recognize her name is because she inspired a chef in San Francisco to create this dish in her honor.

1 broiler-fryer (2½ to 3 lbs.), cut in pieces
2 cups water
1 cup dry white wine
2 carrots, cut in pieces
1 medium-sized onion, chopped
2 sprigs parsley
¼ teaspoon thyme
1½ teaspoons salt
6 tablespoons butter or margarine
5 tablespoons flour
½ cup light cream
¾ cup shredded Parmesan cheese
¾ pound mushrooms, sliced
Salted water
8 ounces noodles (spaghetti or tagliarini)

Place chicken in deep pot and add water, wine, carrots, onion, parsley, thyme, and salt. Bring to a boil, cover, and simmer slowly for about 40 minutes or until chicken is tender. Pour broth through wire strainer and save. When chicken is cool enough to touch, remove skin and bones and discard. Cut meat in thin slivers and set aside.

Melt 2 tablespoons of the butter, mix in flour, and gradually blend in 3¾ cups of the reserved chicken broth (add water if you do not have quite that much broth), and cream. Cook, stirring, for about 3 minutes after sauce begins to simmer. Stir in ½ cup of the cheese. Remove from heat. Measure out 1 cup of the sauce and blend remaining cheese with it.

Melt remaining 4 tablespoons of butter in another pan and cook mushrooms quickly until lightly browned. At same time bring a quantity of salted water to boiling, add noodles and cook until they're just tender to bite, but not soft. Drain noodles and combine with large portion of sauce, the chicken, and mushrooms (save a few nice large slices for garnish).

Pour into a large shallow casserole or individual casseroles. Spoon the reserved 1 cup sauce evenly over surface and top with mushroom garnish.

Bake, uncovered, in a moderately hot oven

Thin slices of lemon, sprigs of mint, and a little brown sugar flavor chicken in Lemon Chicken casserole.

(375°) until bubbling; allow about 15 minutes for large casserole, 8 minutes for small dishes. Broil tops until lightly browned. Makes 6 to 8 servings.

Rock Cornish Game Hen with Pilaf

A savory pilaf base soaks up the rich juices of the game hen as it cooks in this casserole.

1 Rock Cornish game hen, cut in half, and giblets
   if desired
4 tablespoons butter or margarine
½ cup uncooked rice
1 can (4 oz.) mushrooms and liquid
1 cup peas, fresh or frozen
1¼ cups chicken broth, or ¾ cup chicken broth
   and ½ cup light cream
½ teaspoon salt
2 or 3 tablespoons red wine

Sauté game hen in butter until lightly browned (cook cut side first, then skin side); set aside. Add to butter the rice, mushrooms and liquid, peas, broth, and salt. Pour into casserole and place hen halves on top. Cover and bake in a moderate oven (350°) for 30 to 40 minutes or until rice is cooked. Pour red wine over all and serve. Makes 2 servings.

Rock Cornish Game Hen, Basque Style

A rich red pimiento sauce from the Basque country coats this game hen.

1 Rock Cornish game hen and giblets
2 tablespoons butter or margarine
Juice of ½ lemon
Salt
Melted butter or margarine (about 2 tablespoons)
½ medium-sized onion, chopped
1 cup chicken broth
⅓ cup tomato purée
½ bay leaf
⅛ teaspoon oregano
⅛ teaspoon marjoram
⅛ teaspoon thyme
⅛ teaspoon tarragon
⅛ teaspoon basil
¼ cup chopped pimiento
2 tablespoons chopped ripe olives

Pat bird dry and skewer the neck opening closed. Fill cavity with giblets and butter; add lemon juice and sprinkle with salt. Skewer shut abdominal opening. Brush bird with melted butter, and roast in moderate oven (350°) for 30 minutes. Baste with more butter when needed. Remove from oven; set bird aside. Pour drippings (scrape free any residue) into saucepan. Simmer onion until transparent in drippings; add broth, tomato purée, seasonings, pimiento, and olives. Bring to a boil and simmer for about 5 minutes. Cut bird in half along breastbone and backbone and place in shallow casserole (about 9 inches square). Chop giblets, add to sauce; pour sauce over bird and cover. Bake in moderate oven (350°) for 20 minutes; uncover and bake for 10 minutes longer, basting occasionally. Makes 1 or 2 servings.

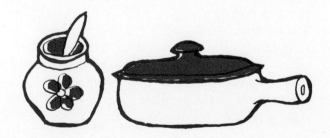

Turkey and Asparagus Supreme

Here is a speedy way to use leftover turkey in a main dish that is special enough for a guest buffet.

1 quart (4 cups) sliced leftover turkey
3 packages frozen cut asparagus, cooked, or 2 cans (1 lb. each) asparagus spears, cut in 1-inch lengths
3 cups hot medium-thick cream sauce (6 tablespoons butter, 6 tablespoons flour, 2½ cups milk)
1 cup mayonnaise
3 to 4 cups hot cooked rice

In a greased shallow casserole (about 9 by 13 inches), arrange half the turkey in a layer, cover with asparagus, and top with remaining turkey. While cream sauce is hot, stir in mayonnaise; let cool. Spoon sauce over layered casserole and run a knife through to bottom in several places to distribute sauce. Bake, uncovered, in a hot oven (400°) for 20 minutes. Serve over hot rice. Makes 6 servings.

Wild Rice and Turkey Casserole

Wild rice gives distinction to this casserole. You might serve it garnished on top with butter-sautéed mushrooms and canned pimiento strips.

¾ cup wild rice
Boiling salted water
½ pound pork sausage meat
1 can (3 or 4 oz.) sliced mushrooms
1 can (10½ oz.) cream of mushroom soup
About 1 pound turkey slices

Cook wild rice in boiling salted water as directed on package; drain if needed. Cook sausage meat, breaking it up with a fork, until browned lightly all over. Drain mushroom liquid into undiluted mushroom soup. In a buttered 2-quart casserole, layer half the cooked wild rice; top with a layer using half the cooked sausage. Spread half the mushroom slices over sausage, then arrange half the turkey slices. Pour half the mushroom soup mixture over turkey. Then repeat layers, using remaining ingredients. Cover and bake in moderately hot oven (375°) about 30 minutes, or until bubbly. Makes 4 servings.

Turkey Custard Casserole

A nest of stuffing, a generous layer of turkey, and a covering of delicately spiced custard add up to a delicious and filling casserole.

3 cups leftover bread stuffing
2 cups sliced cooked turkey
1 tablespoon minced onion
2 tablespoons butter
2 tablespoons flour
2 cups broth made from turkey giblets or chicken stock
½ teaspoon thyme
¼ teaspoon ground ginger
¼ teaspoon nutmeg
Salt and black pepper
2 eggs, well-beaten
2 tablespoons fine dry bread crumbs mixed with 1 tablespoon melted butter

Butter a 2½-quart casserole; line sides and bottom with stuffing and arrange sliced turkey in a layer over the stuffing. Set aside and make sauce as follows:

Sauté onions in butter, then stir in flour and cook until bubbly. Gradually stir in broth and seasonings, bring to a boil, stirring constantly. Slowly pour mixture into beaten eggs, stirring to mix well. Cool. Pour carefully into lined casserole; sprinkle with crumbs. Place casserole in pan of hot water and bake, uncovered, in a moderately hot oven (375°) for 45 minutes or until top is set. Serve with cranberry or grape jelly. Makes 6 to 8 servings.

Turkey and Sausage Casserole

Sausage and almonds with turkey create a casserole that is faintly reminiscent of a holiday bird stuffing. This is a large-quantity recipe, so you may want to divide the mixture and freeze half for later use.

½ pound pork sausage meat
1 cup chopped celery
1 cup chopped onion
1 cup uncooked rice
3 cans (10½ oz. each) chicken noodle soup
1½ cups water
½ cup blanched almonds, sliced
2 cups sliced cooked turkey
1 cup crushed potato chips

Sauté sausage, celery, and onion until meat is browned. Combine with rice, soup, water, almonds, and sliced turkey in a 3-quart casserole. Cover. Bake in moderately slow oven (325°) for 1½ hours. Remove cover for last 20 minutes and top with crushed potato chips; continue baking. Makes 8 to 10 servings. To bake a smaller casserole, reduce time to about 1 hour.

Turkey and Oyster Casserole

Turkey meat stored in your freezer provides the basic ingredient for this casserole. You might add a garnish of toast triangles, heaped with cranberry sauce.

1 package (8 oz.) broad noodles
1½ cups sour cream
5 tablespoons butter or margarine
5 tablespoons flour
2 cups turkey broth or chicken stock
3 cups diced cooked turkey
½ cup chopped pimientos
½ cup sliced ripe olives
1 can (3 or 4 oz.) sliced mushrooms, drained
1 teaspoon salt
¼ teaspoon pepper
1 pint oysters, drained

Cook noodles as directed on package; drain. Mix the cooked noodles with ½ cup of the sour cream. Melt butter in a small pan, blend in flour, and gradually stir in turkey broth. Cook, stirring, until thickened; blend in the remaining sour cream. Stir into the noodles with the turkey, pimientos, olives, mushrooms, salt, pepper. Turn half of the mixture into a greased 2-quart casserole. Arrange a layer of oysters, then cover with remaining noodle mixture. Bake, uncovered, in a moderate oven (350°) about 30 minutes. Makes 6 to 8 servings.

Turkey Puff

Toasted almonds add crunchiness to this turkey or chicken casserole that has a fluffy cheese and egg topping.

½ cup finely chopped onion
½ cup diced celery
2 tablespoons butter or margarine
2 cups cooked turkey or chicken
1 can (10½ oz.) chicken noodle soup
½ cup light cream
1 can (2 or 3 oz.) mushroom slices or pieces, drained
2 tablespoons diced pimiento
½ cup slivered toasted almonds
½ teaspoon salt
½ teaspoon freshly ground pepper
4 eggs, separated
½ cup shredded Cheddar cheese

In a large pan, sauté the onion and celery in butter. Add the turkey, soup, cream, mushrooms, pimiento, almonds, salt, and pepper; blend well. Cook over low heat just until hot. Pour into a buttered 2-quart casserole. Beat the egg yolks, add cheese; fold in egg whites, beaten until stiff, but not dry. Pour egg-cheese mixture over top of casserole. Bake, uncovered, in a moderate oven (350°) for 30 minutes. Makes 6 servings.

Wild Rice and Shrimp Casserole (page 52) is an elegant cook-ahead casserole for a buffet. Perfect companions are papaya wedges with lime, butterflake rolls, white wine.

Sea Food Casseroles

Wonderful ways with fish and shellfish

Amber Curried Crab with Tomato

This crab curry sauce gives a rich flavor to the bed of steamy rice in the bottom of the individual servings. If you choose to bake the curry in a single serving dish, simply serve the sauce over hot fluffy rice.

2 tablespoons butter or margarine, melted
1 tablespoon curry powder
1 medium-sized onion, chopped fine
¼ cup finely sliced celery
½ can (6 oz. size) tomato paste
1 cup water
1 tablespoon sugar
1 teaspoon garlic salt
Salt and pepper to taste
1½ cups uncooked long grain rice
1 pound crab meat
2 medium-sized tomatoes, thinly sliced
6 tablespoons white wine vinegar
1 hard-cooked egg, finely chopped

Add to butter in a small saucepan the curry, onion, and celery, and cook about 3 minutes. Stir in tomato paste, water, sugar, garlic salt, salt, and pepper.

Cook and stir 2 to 3 minutes longer. Place ¼ cup uncooked rice in bottom of each of 6 buttered individual casseroles. Arrange half the crab meat over rice in each casserole, add a layer of half the sauce, then a layer of half the sliced tomatoes. Repeat layering with remaining crab, sauce, and sliced tomatoes. Sprinkle 1 tablespoon vinegar over top of each casserole. Bake, uncovered, in moderate oven (350°) for 25 minutes. Just before serving, sprinkle with hard-cooked eggs. Makes 6 servings.

Crab-Rice-Cheese Casserole

This casserole needs no more seasoning than wine, but is quite receptive to other subtle additions. Use any seasonings that are compatible with shellfish and cheese. If you want to make it really luxurious, increase the amount of crab.

½ teaspoon salt
3 cups water
1½ cups uncooked rice
3 tablespoons flour
¼ cup (⅛ lb.) butter, melted
1 cup milk
1 cup shredded Cheddar cheese
Pepper
½ cup sherry or dry white wine
2 hard-cooked eggs, diced
½ pound (or more) crab meat
Shredded Cheddar cheese
Pimiento strips (optional)

Bring salted water to a boil in a heavy pan with lid. Add rice, cover, decrease heat, and steam for 15 minutes. (Do not uncover during cooking!)

Meanwhile, prepare cheese sauce as follows: Stir flour into melted butter. Gradually add milk and cook while stirring with a whisk until mixture is thick. Add the 1 cup cheese and stir until cheese is melted. Taste and add more salt if needed (also pepper and other seasoning if desired). Remove from heat and stir in wine.

Combine rice, sauce, diced eggs, and crab meat. Place in buttered casserole dish (about 2-quart size) and cover with a little more shredded Cheddar cheese. Decorate top with pimiento strips. Bake 30 minutes in moderate oven (350°). Cook longer if you prefer a more crusty effect. Makes 4 to 6 servings.

Crab and Spinach Casserole

Crab and spinach make surprisingly good casserole mates. The nutmeg is an apt addition, but take care that the dash does not become a deluge, for the taste comes through very strongly in this dish.

2 pounds fresh or 2 packages (10 oz. each) frozen spinach
¼ pound sharp Cheddar cheese, shredded
1 pound crab meat
1 tablespoon scraped onion (optional)
1 tablespoon lemon juice
Dash of nutmeg
1 tablespoon flour
2 tablespoons butter, melted
½ can (10½ oz. size) tomato soup
½ pint sour cream

Cook spinach about 1 minute in small amount of water; drain thoroughly and chop. Arrange in bottom of greased 1½-quart casserole. Sprinkle with half the cheese, then crab meat and onion, if used. Add lemon juice and dash of nutmeg. Blend flour in butter; add soup and cook until slightly thickened. Remove from heat; stir in sour cream and pour over spinach mixture. Sprinkle with remaining half of cheese. Bake, uncovered, in moderate oven (350°) for 30 minutes. Makes 6 servings.

Crab and Avocado Casserole

Only occasionally does one find a recipe that produces such elegant results with such a simple combination of ingredients.

1 tablespoon butter
2 medium-sized avocados, peeled and sliced
½ pound crab meat (about 2 cups)
3 tablespoons lemon juice
½ teaspoon salt
½ teaspoon pepper
1 can (10½ oz.) cream of mushroom soup
1 cup crumbs from grated frozen bread (or 1 cup well packed soft bread crumbs) mixed with 2 tablespoons melted butter

Generously grease a 2-quart casserole with the 1 tablespoon butter. Arrange avocado in casserole in alternate layers with crab meat. Top each layer with part of lemon, salt, and pepper. Over the top pour undiluted mushroom soup. Sprinkle buttered bread crumbs over top. Bake in moderate oven (350°) for 20 minutes, or until just heated through. Baking time and temperature must be carefully controlled for this casserole, for avocado is delicious when just heated, but becomes bitter if overcooked. Makes 4 servings.

Crab Giovanni

When preparation time for a special dinner is a problem, this hearty crab casserole may be just the answer. It is easy to put together and may be refrigerated one or two days before it is baked.

2 cups chopped onions
½ pound fresh mushrooms, sliced
2 cloves garlic, minced or mashed
½ cup (¼ lb.) butter or margarine, melted
½ pound spaghetti or vermicelli, cooked
2 to 3 cups crab meat
½ cup sliced stuffed green olives
½ pound shredded sharp Cheddar cheese
½ cup sour cream
1 large can (1 lb., 12 oz.) tomatoes, broken in pieces
1½ teaspoons salt
½ teaspoon basil

In a large frying pan, slowly sauté the onions, mushrooms, and garlic in butter until tender. Combine with remaining ingredients, stirring until well mixed. Pour mixture into greased 3-quart casserole or baking dish and bake, uncovered, in moderate oven (350°) for 35 to 45 minutes, or until hot and bubbly. (If the dish has been refrigerated, allow about 1 hour's baking time.) Makes 8 to 10 servings.

Crab Salad Casserole (see suggested menu below) *

1 pound (about 2 cups) crab meat, or 1 cup
  crab meat and 1 large can (9½ oz.)
  flaked tuna, drained
1 cup sliced celery
½ cup finely chopped green pepper
2 hard-cooked eggs, chopped
2½ tablespoons Worcestershire
1 cup mayonnaise
¾ cup fine soft bread crumbs, mixed
  with about 2 tablespoons melted butter

Combine crab meat, or crab meat and tuna, with celery, green pepper, eggs, Worcestershire, and mayonnaise; mix together with a fork. Turn into baking dish (about 1½ quart); top with buttered bread crumbs. Heat, uncovered, in moderately slow oven (325°) for 30 minutes. Makes 6 servings.

---

* Family Lenten Supper

Cream of Tomato Soup Sprinkled with
Parmesan Cheese
Crab Salad Casserole (see recipe above)
Warm Rye Slices with Mustard Butter
Coconut-Lemon Sponge Pudding

The crab entrée in this menu is much like a hot salad. The casserole, bread, and lemon sponge pudding can all go into the oven at the same time; the pudding continues to bake while you're eating the first part of the meal.

Warm Rye Slices with Mustard Butter

Thickly slice a loaf of sour rye bread with caraway. Generously butter each slice with mustard spread made by blending ¼ cup (⅛ pound) soft butter with 1 teaspoon prepared mustard and a dash of cayenne. Put slices back together in a loaf shape; wrap in foil. Heat for 30 minutes in a moderately slow oven (325°).

Coconut-Lemon Sponge Pudding

3 eggs, separated
¾ cup sugar
1 cup milk
2 tablespoons flour
Grated peel and juice of 2 large lemons
⅛ teaspoon salt
½ cup flaked coconut
¼ cup sugar

Beat egg yolks with the ¾ cup sugar, milk, flour, lemon peel and juice, and salt. Stir in coconut. Beat egg whites with the ¼ cup sugar until stiff but not dry. Fold into coconut mixture. Turn into a greased baking dish (about 2-quart size). Set in a pan of hot water, and bake in a moderately hot oven (325°) for 55 minutes or until pudding is puffed and brown. Spoon into serving dishes, ladling lemon sauce from bottom of baking dish over spongy portion. Makes 8 servings.

Crab Casserole with Artichoke Hearts

A gay pottery container seems to suit this delicious casserole. Serve it with tossed green salad, French dressing, and your favorite hot bread.

3 tablespoons flour
3 tablespoons butter or margarine, melted
1 cup milk
½ cup white wine or chicken broth
½ cup shredded medium sharp Cheddar or
  Swiss cheese
2 teaspoons Worcestershire
2 packages (9 oz. each) frozen artichoke hearts,
  cooked and drained
4 hard-cooked eggs, sliced
¾ pound crab meat
2 tablespoons grated Parmesan cheese

Mix flour with melted butter in saucepan and gradually stir in 1 cup milk. Cook until thickened, stirring constantly. Slowly blend in wine or broth. Add cheese and Worcestershire; cook until cheese melts.

Spoon a little sauce in bottom of 1½-quart casserole. Alternate layers of cooked and drained artichoke hearts (reserving a few of nicest for garnish), eggs, and crab meat. Make a middle layer of half the sauce, and top casserole with remaining sauce. Sprinkle with Parmesan cheese.

At this point you can refrigerate the casserole until you're ready to bake, uncovered, in moderate oven (350°) for 30 minutes. Garnish with crab legs and artichoke hearts just before serving. Makes 4 or 5 servings.

Layers of artichoke hearts, egg slices, crab meat alternate in a rich cheese sauce. Keep accompaniments simple—a green salad and your favorite hot bread or rolls.

Rosy Baked Crab

Scallop shells or large clam shells are ideal for baking individual servings of this colorful crab, but it may also be baked in a casserole.

2 tablespoons flour
2 tablespoons butter or margarine, melted
¾ cup condensed tomato soup
1 tablespoon grated onion and juice
¼ cup chopped green pepper
2 tablespoons finely chopped celery
2 tablespoons finely chopped parsley
½ teaspoon salt
¼ teaspoon pepper
1 teaspoon paprika
2 cups crab meat
⅔ cup mayonnaise
¼ cup fine dry bread crumbs mixed
  with 1 tablespoon melted butter

Blend flour in butter and cook until bubbly. Gradually stir in undiluted tomato soup. Stir over medium heat until thickened. Add onion, green pepper, celery, parsley, and seasonings. Cook about 1 minute. Remove from heat and stir in crab meat and mayonnaise. Spoon the mixture into buttered individual shells or into 1-quart casserole. Sprinkle top with buttered bread crumbs. Bake in moderate oven (350°) about 15 minutes or until crumbs are lightly browned. Makes about 6 servings.

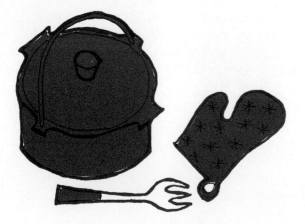

Deviled Crab with Avocados

This attractive crab and avocado entrée is especially suitable for a luncheon or supper. If you have a special set of individual oven-proof casseroles or ramekins, you might use them for baking and serving this dish.

2 ripe avocados, peeled and halved (cut into
    thirds or quarters for smaller servings)
¼ cup white wine vinegar
2 small cloves garlic, cut in pieces
¼ cup (⅛ lb.) butter or margarine
3 tablespoons flour
1½ cups milk
2 cups crab meat
½ teaspoon prepared mustard
1½ teaspoons salt
2 tablespoons lemon juice
1 teaspoon Worcestershire
1 tablespoon minced parsley (or 1 teaspoon
    dried parsley)
⅓ cup shredded American or Cheddar cheese
Dash of paprika

Fill the hollows of the avocados with the vinegar and place a piece of garlic in each; let stand about 30 minutes. Meanwhile, melt butter, add flour and stir to blend well over medium heat. Add milk gradually, stirring constantly until mixture is thickened. Stir in crab, mustard, salt, lemon juice, Worcestershire, and parsley.

Pour off vinegar from avocados and discard pieces of garlic. Arrange avocado pieces in a 3-quart baking dish or in individual casseroles. Spoon hot crab mixture over avocado, using all the sauce. Sprinkle shredded cheese over sauce and top with dash of paprika. Place in moderately slow oven (325°) until avocados are just heated through and cheese is melted, about 7 to 10 minutes. Do not overbake as avocados will lose their good flavor. Makes 4 to 6 servings.

Shellfish Casserole

This casserole goes together quickly.

1 cup vegetable juice cocktail or tomato juice
1 cup mayonnaise
1 can (7 or 8 oz.) crab meat or 1 to 1½ cups
    fresh crab meat
1 can (about 5 oz.) shrimp or 1 cup small
    fresh shrimp (shelled and deveined)
2 cups cooked rice
⅓ cup chopped green pepper
Salt and pepper to taste
2 tablespoons butter, melted
1 cup fresh bread crumbs
½ cup slivered almonds

In a bowl, combine the vegetable juice and mayonnaise; mix until well blended. Stir in crab meat, shrimp, rice, green pepper, and salt and pepper to taste; mix just until ingredients are well distributed. Spoon into greased 2-quart casserole.

In small pan, add to butter the fresh bread crumbs and almonds. Mix with fork until crumbs are coated with butter. Spoon evenly over mixture in the casserole. Bake in moderately hot oven (375°) until bubbly and top is lightly browned. Serve immediately. Makes about 6 to 8 servings.

Scalloped Clams

Here is a casserole version of clam chowder.

4 slices bacon
1 small onion, minced
2 cans (7½ oz. each) minced clams, drained,
    or 2 cups fresh minced clams
8 soda crackers, crushed
1 egg, slightly beaten
¾ cup milk

Fry bacon until crisp; lift bacon out of pan and drain. Add the onion to the bacon fat in the pan, and cook slowly until golden brown. Stir in the clams and crackers. Combine egg with milk and stir into the clam mixture. Turn into a well greased 1-quart baking dish. Crumble the bacon over the top. Let the casserole stand at room temperature for 15 minutes, then bake, uncovered, in moderate oven (350°) for about 20 minutes. Makes 3 or 4 servings.

Haddock Casserole

In this casserole, haddock tastes almost like crab. The sauce is enriched with sour cream and sharp cheese.

2 pounds frozen haddock fillets
Water
¼ cup (⅛ lb.) butter or margarine
4 tablespoons (¼ cup) flour
2 cups milk
1 cup (¼ lb.) shredded sharp Cheddar cheese
½ pound fresh mushrooms, sliced
1 small onion, minced
2 tablespoons salad oil
1 package (10 oz.) frozen peas, cooked and drained
1 cup (½ pint) sour cream
Salt and pepper

Barely cover haddock with water and simmer gently for 15 minutes, or until fish flakes with a fork; drain, and flake meat in large chunks. While fish is cooking, melt butter; blend in flour. Add milk, and stirring, cook over low heat until smooth and thick. Add cheese and cook until it melts; remove sauce from heat.

Sauté mushrooms and onion in salad oil for 5 minutes; add to cream sauce, along with cooked peas, sour cream, and flaked fish. Mix lightly, add salt and pepper to taste, and turn into a shallow 3-quart casserole or baking dish. Heat under the broiler until bubbly and lightly browned on top. Makes 8 servings.

Halibut Casserole Espagnol

Here is a good treatment for halibut or any other rather bland white fish.

1 medium-sized onion, minced
¼ cup minced green pepper
1 cup chopped celery
2 tablespoons salad oil or butter
1 can (10½ oz.) tomato soup and 1 can water
½ teaspoon salt
1 teaspoon curry powder
1 tablespoon Worcestershire
1 teaspoon lemon juice
1 teaspoon tarragon vinegar
1 teaspoon coarse ground black pepper
1 teaspoon sweet basil or oregano
1 teaspoon marjoram
1 pulverized chili tepine
2 pounds cooked halibut, flaked
1 cup cooked wild rice or dry bread crumbs
¼ pound shredded sharp Cheddar cheese

Sauté onion, green pepper, and celery in oil until soft but not brown. Add tomato soup and the can of water. Then add salt, curry powder, Worcestershire, lemon juice, tarragon vinegar, black pepper, sweet basil or oregano, marjoram, chili tepine; let ingredients blend 15 minutes or so.

Place halibut in large bowl and add previous mixture together with the cup of wild rice, blending well. Place in greased 2-quart casserole. Cover and bake in a moderate oven (350°) for about 30 minutes, until heated through. Add shredded cheese as topping and put casserole under broiler until cheese is slightly brown. Makes 4 to 6 servings.

Baked Halibut with Limas

A fish and vegetable combination is a good company meal because it simplifies serving. This combination of lima beans and halibut bakes so quickly that the beans keep part of their crunchiness.

1 clove garlic, mashed or minced
1 small onion, finely chopped

1 can (3 or 4 oz.) sliced mushrooms, drained
¼ cup (⅛ lb.) butter or margarine
2 tablespoons flour
1 can (1 lb.) tomatoes
2 tablespoons vinegar
1 tablespoon Worcestershire
1 teaspoon salt
¼ teaspoon thyme
Pepper
1 package (10 oz.) frozen lima beans
2 pounds halibut fillets or steaks, cut ¾ inch thick

Sauté garlic, onion, and mushrooms in butter for 5 minutes; add flour and blend until smooth. Add tomatoes, vinegar, Worcestershire, salt, thyme, and dash of pepper; stirring, cook until slightly thickened. Place frozen limas in tomato sauce, and cook just until beans are separated, about 5 minutes. Arrange fish in single layer in greased baking pan (about 9 by 13 inches); pour over tomato and lima bean sauce. Cover and bake in hot oven (400°) for 30 minutes, or until fish flakes with fork. Makes 6 servings.

Rice and Oyster Bake

This combination of rice, vegetables, and shellfish is reminiscent of Spanish *paellas*. You might add the oyster liquid to the water in which you cook the rice to more fully duplicate the European custom of cooking rice in stock.

1 cup uncooked brown rice
2 cups salted water
½ cup (¼ lb.) butter or margarine
1 cup chopped onions
1 pound fresh mushrooms, thinly sliced
1½ teaspoons seasoned salt
1 cup dry white wine
2 cans (8 oz. each) oysters or 1 pint fresh oysters
⅛ teaspoon freshly ground pepper

Cook rice in boiling salted water for 40 minutes, or until tender. Melt half the butter in a pan; add the onions and mushrooms and sauté slowly for about 10 minutes. Sprinkle with half the seasoned salt, pour in wine, and simmer 5 minutes. Combine mushroom sauce with rice and turn into a buttered 3-quart casserole. Melt remaining ¼ cup butter; dip each oyster in the butter and

arrange over top of rice mixture. Sprinkle with remaining seasoned salt and the pepper. Bake, uncovered, in moderate oven (350°) for 30 minutes. Makes 6 servings.

Salmon Lasagne Casserole

Though it borrows the long, flat noodles from the popular Italian *lasagne*, this dish has a flavor all its own.

¼ cup chopped onion
⅓ cup chopped green pepper
2 tablespoons butter or margarine
1 can (6 oz.) tomato paste
¾ cup water
½ teaspoon salt
Dash of pepper
½ teaspoon basil
1 can (1 lb.) salmon, drained, skinned, and flaked
¼ pound lasagne noodles, cooked until tender
4 ounces Mozzarella cheese, sliced thinly
¼ cup grated Parmesan cheese

Sauté onion and green pepper in butter until tender. Add tomato paste, water, salt, pepper, basil, and salmon; stir until blended. In a greased 9-inch-square baking dish or casserole, make a layer of the noodles. Top with some of the salmon mixture, then both kinds of cheese. Repeat layers of noodles, salmon, and cheese, ending with a layer of cheese on top. Bake, uncovered, in a moderately hot oven (375°) for 25 to 30 minutes, or until bubbly and browned. Makes 6 servings.

Salmon Casserole with Caraway

The flavor of caraway seed distinguishes this salmon dish.

2 eggs
½ cup non-fat dry milk
1 teaspoon salt
¼ teaspoon pepper
1 cup milk
1 can (1 lb.) salmon, drained, skinned, and flaked
¼ cup finely chopped parsley
¼ cup finely chopped onion
½ cup finely sliced celery, including leaves
1 teaspoon caraway seed
1 cup shredded Cheddar cheese

Mix together eggs and dry milk until smooth. Stir in salt, pepper, and milk. Add salmon, parsley, onion, celery and leaves, and caraway seed, and mix thoroughly. Turn into greased 1½-quart casserole. Sprinkle top with shredded cheese. Bake, uncovered, in moderate oven (350°) for 30 minutes, or until set. Makes 6 servings.

Rice and Salmon Bake

This colorful casserole of salmon and rice is a good menu choice when you have a busy schedule.

2 cups flaked cooked salmon, or 1 can (1 lb.) salmon, skinned, drained, and flaked
1 small green pepper, cut in strips ¼ inch wide and 1 inch long
3 small stalks celery, sliced diagonally
1 medium-sized onion, chopped
3 tomatoes, peeled and chopped
¾ cup uncooked rice
1 can (10½ oz.) mushroom soup
1 soup can water
1 tablespoon soy sauce

Combine salmon with green pepper, celery, onion, tomatoes, rice, mushroom soup, water, and soy sauce. Mix well, then turn into a lightly greased 2-quart casserole. Cover and bake in a moderate oven (350°) for 1 hour. Makes 4 to 6 servings.

Salmon and Green Olive Casserole

This casserole, made from canned salmon, has enough distinction to star at a buffet.

2 tablespoons chopped shallots or green onions
¼ cup (⅛ lb.) butter
¼ cup flour
Freshly ground pepper
1 can (1 lb.) salmon
About 1¾ cups light cream
½ cup diced green olives
2 teaspoons dill weed
Salt
¼ cup soft bread crumbs, mixed with 1 tablespoon melted butter

Sauté shallots or green onions in butter until wilted. Stir in flour and about 2 grindings of the pepper mill. Drain salmon, reserving liquid. Add enough light cream to salmon liquid to make 2 cups; stir into flour mixture. Cook, stirring, until thick and smooth. Add olives, dill weed, and salt, if necessary. Remove skin and bone from salmon, break into large pieces and place in a 1-quart casserole. Pour in the sauce, turn 2 or 3 times with fork to mix, and sprinkle top with buttered crumbs. Before serving, heat in hot oven (400°) for 15 minutes, or until hot and brown on top. Makes 6 servings.

Salmon and Oysters en Casserole *(see suggested menu below)* ✲

2 cans (1 lb. each) red salmon, drained, skinned,
   and broken in chunks
2 jars (about 12 oz. each) oysters
Butter or margarine
¾ cup flour
½ cup (¼ lb.) butter or margarine, melted
4 cups milk (or substitute 1 cup sherry for 1 cup
   of the milk)
1 teaspoon sweet basil
2 teaspoons salt
1 teaspoon pepper
2 teaspoons monosodium glutamate
2 tablespoons lemon juice
2 cups shredded Cheddar cheese (about ½ lb.)
Thin tomato slices
Small Cheddar cheese slices

Arrange salmon in bottom of buttered 3-quart casserole. Poach oysters in their liquid until edges curl; add butter if needed. Drain liquid and reserve. Place oysters over salmon.

Stir flour into the ½ cup melted butter to make a smooth paste. Gradually add milk, then reserved oyster liquid, sweet basil, salt, pepper, monosodium glutamate, and lemon juice. Add the shredded cheese, and heat until sauce is thick and smooth and cheese is melted. Pour sauce over salmon and oysters. Bake, uncovered, in moderate oven (350°) about 30 minutes. Just before serving arrange tomato slices, topped with small cheese slices, over top of casserole; broil until cheese melts. Serve over crisp toast, if desired. Makes 8 servings.

✲ Seafood Supper Party

Tomato-topped Salmon and Oysters en Casserole *(see recipe above)*
Marinated Broccoli   Crisp Sesame Rounds
Spiced Cherry Compote   Wafer Cookies

You can assemble the casserole in its baking and serving container as much as a day ahead. Before the party, just bake and garnish. Prepare the broccoli about an hour early and slip it into the refrigerator to marinate.

Marinated Broccoli

Cook 3 pounds fresh broccoli in boiling salted water until tender (about 10 minutes). Drain and cool. Marinate in a sharp French dressing for at least 1 hour; drain and arrange on a serving plate with a lemon-wedge garnish. Makes 8 to 10 servings.

Crisp Sesame Rounds

Break apart biscuits from 2 packages refrigerator biscuits. Press each into a round; dip one side into sesame seed, which you have generously sprinkled on a board. Turn and coat the other side with seed; roll out to ⅛-inch thickness. Place on well-greased baking sheet. Bake in a hot oven (400°) for 10 minutes or until brown and crisp. Makes 20 rounds.

Spiced Cherry Compote

3 cans (1 lb. each) sour pitted cherries
Water
1½ cups sugar
1 tablespoon cinnamon
3 lemons, thinly sliced
1½ teaspoons almond extract
Few drops red food coloring

Drain cherries, reserving liquid. Measure liquid and add enough water to make 2 cups. Combine liquid with sugar, cinnamon, lemons (reserve a few slices for garnish); simmer, uncovered, until syrup is reduced one-half. Add almond extract, cherries, red food coloring, and remaining lemon slices. Heat through. Makes 8 to 10 servings.

Salmon Pudding (see suggested menu below) ✳

2 pounds boneless fresh salmon,
  cut in 1-inch cubes
3 cups cooked rice (1 cup uncooked rice)
1 small onion, chopped
2 tablespoons butter
3 eggs
1 teaspoon salt
¼ teaspoon freshly ground black pepper
¼ teaspoon thyme
3 cups milk
Melted butter

Combine salmon with rice and put in a well-greased 2 or 2½-quart casserole. Cook onion in the 2 tablespoons butter until wilted. Beat eggs with the salt, pepper, thyme, and milk. Add onion, and pour over the mixture in the casserole. Bake in a moderate oven (350°) for 45 to 50 minutes, or until set. Serve with a small pitcher of melted butter. Makes 6 generous servings.

✳ A Springtime Supper

Salmon Pudding (see recipe above)
Asparagus with Bacon and Egg Sauce
Hard Rolls
Lemon Cheese Pie

This supper takes advantage of two spring favorites—fresh salmon and fresh asparagus.

Asparagus with Bacon and Egg Sauce

4 slices bacon
2 green onions, finely chopped
¼ cup tarragon vinegar
2 pounds asparagus, sliced in very thin
  diagonal slices
Boiling salted water
3 hard-cooked eggs, chopped

Fry bacon until crisp; remove bacon from fat; drain and crumble. Add onions to bacon fat, and sauté until wilted; stir in vinegar. Cook asparagus in a small amount of boiling salted water for 3 minutes—no longer. Drain and put in a heated serving dish. Sprinkle chopped eggs on top, then crumbled bacon, and finally pour hot vinegar mixture over all. Makes 6 servings.

Lemon Cheese Pie

1 cup regular all-purpose flour
½ teaspoon salt
⅓ cup shortening
1 egg, slightly beaten
1 teaspoon grated lemon peel
1 tablespoon lemon juice

Lemon cheese filling:
1¼ cups sugar
¼ cup cornstarch
1 cup water
1 teaspoon grated lemon peel
⅓ cup lemon juice
2 eggs, separated
½ cup (4 oz.) cream cheese

Sift flour, measure, and sift again with salt into a bowl. Cut in shortening until fine. Combine egg with lemon peel and juice; sprinkle over flour mixture. Toss with a fork until the dough holds together. Roll out to fit a deep 9-inch pie pan. Flute edge, prick, bake in a hot oven (400°) for 12 to 15 minutes. Cool.

For the filling, combine 1 cup of the sugar with cornstarch. Stir in water, lemon peel and juice, and egg yolks, beaten. Cook, stirring, until thick. Remove from heat; blend in cream cheese. Cool. Beat egg whites to soft peaks; gradually beat in remaining ¼ cup sugar. Fold into lemon mixture. Turn into pie shell. Chill.

Salmon-Cheese Casserole

A layer of cheese custard bakes on top of the salmon in this easy casserole.

1½ cups milk
2 tablespoons butter or margarine
1 cup soft bread crumbs
3 eggs, well beaten
2 tablespoons minced parsley
2 tablespoons finely chopped onions
1½ cups shredded sharp Cheddar cheese
⅛ teaspoon pepper
Dash paprika
1 can (1 lb.) salmon, drained, skinned, and broken in pieces

Heat milk and butter together until butter is melted. Stir bread crumbs into eggs; then stir in hot milk. Add parsley, onion, cheese, pepper, and paprika, and mix until well blended. Spread salmon in bottom of greased 1½-quart casserole. Pour custard mixture over salmon. Set casserole in larger pan of hot water and bake, uncovered, in moderate oven (350°) for about 1 hour, or until custard is set. Serve hot. Makes 4 to 6 servings.

Smoked Fish and Rice Casserole

Serve this flavorful rice casserole for a family dinner. You can assemble it ahead of dinner time, if you wish.

2 cups cooked rice (brown rice or regular rice)
1 pound smoked fish, flaked and bones removed
1 cup cooked peas
1 medium-sized onion, chopped
2 tablespoons butter or margarine
1 can (8 oz.) tomato sauce
1 egg, slightly beaten
⅛ teaspoon paprika
⅛ teaspoon nutmeg
¼ cup milk
½ cup shredded Cheddar cheese
Sliced, stuffed green olives (optional)

Combine rice with flaked fish and the peas. Sauté onion in butter until soft, about 5 minutes. Add onion to fish mixture with tomato sauce, egg, paprika, and nutmeg. Stir in milk until blended. Turn mixture into greased, 1½-quart casserole. Sprinkle top with shredded cheese. Bake, uncovered, in moderate oven (350°) until heated and bubbly, about 30 minutes, or a little longer if casserole was assembled ahead and refrigerated before baking. Arrange sliced olives on casserole before serving if you wish. Makes 4 servings.

Shrimp Custard Casserole

This custard-type casserole retains its firmness even after you cut it into wedges or squares to serve.

6 slices white bread (crusts removed, buttered, cubed)
½ pound sharp Cheddar cheese, shredded (about 2 cups)
½ pound cleaned, cooked shrimp or 2 cans (5 oz. each) shrimp
¼ teaspoon dry mustard
3 eggs, slightly beaten
2 cups milk
1 teaspoon salt
⅛ teaspoon pepper
⅛ teaspoon paprika
Few grains cayenne

Arrange half the bread cubes in the bottom of a greased, 9-inch round or square baking dish. Sprinkle with half the cheese, shrimp, and mustard. Make a second layer of the remaining bread, shrimp, and mustard, and top with remaining cheese. Combine eggs, milk, salt, pepper, paprika, and cayenne. Pour over bread and shrimp layers. Place baking dish in pan of hot water and bake, uncovered, in moderately slow oven (325°) for 40 minutes, or until firm. Makes 6 servings.

Wild Rice and Shrimp Casserole

Such choice foods as wild rice, seafood, and plump mushroom caps are combined in wine sauce in this casserole that is suitable for a company buffet.

2 cups wild rice
Boiling salted water
4 tablespoons (⅛ pound) butter or margarine
1 onion, finely chopped
1 pound medium-sized mushrooms
Juice of ½ lemon
2 tablespoons flour
1¼ cups chicken stock
½ cup dry white wine
½ teaspoon salt
¼ teaspoon garlic salt
¼ teaspoon crumbled dried tarragon
3 tablespoons grated Parmesan cheese
1 pound cooked medium-sized shrimp (shelled and de-veined)
⅓ pound crab legs
1 tablespoon finely chopped parsley

Turn rice into a large strainer and wash thoroughly under cold running water. Let soak in water to cover for 1 hour; drain. Cook in boiling salted water for 25 minutes, or until almost tender; drain.

Meanwhile melt 2 tablespoons of the butter in a large frying pan, add onion, and sauté until golden. Wash mushrooms and slice off the stem end, leaving caps whole. Add mushroom caps and stems to the pan and sprinkle with the lemon juice. Cook gently, stirring occasionally, until mushrooms are tender. In another pan melt the remaining 2 tablespoons butter and blend in flour, mixing to make a roux. Pour in the chicken stock and wine; cook, stirring constantly, until thickened. Season with salt, garlic salt, and tarragon, and stir in the Parmesan cheese.

Mix together three-fourths of the sauce, the wild rice, mushrooms, and seafood, reserving a few shrimp and crab legs for garnish. Spoon into a buttered 2-quart casserole, arrange the reserved seafood decoratively on top, and spoon over the remaining sauce. (If you are making this ahead, refrigerate it at this point.) Cover and bake in a moderate oven (350°) for 20 minutes (30 to 35 minutes if casserole was refrigerated). Sprinkle with parsley just before serving. Makes 8 to 10 servings.

Shrimp with Artichoke Hearts

This delicious, crumb-topped casserole is especially quick to assemble.

1 small onion, finely chopped
¼ cup (⅛ lb.) butter or margarine, melted
3 tablespoons flour
About 1¼ cups milk
1 can (3 or 4 oz.) sliced mushrooms, drained with liquid reserved
½ teaspoon salt
⅛ teaspoon pepper
1 teaspoon Worcestershire
1 to 1½ cups cooked shrimp (fresh, frozen, or canned)
12 cooked artichoke hearts (fresh, frozen, or canned)
½ cup fresh bread crumbs, mixed with 1½ tablespoons melted butter

Add onion to the ¼ cup melted butter and sauté until soft and yellow. Stir in flour until well blended. Add milk to mushroom liquid to make 1½ cups liquid. Gradually add this liquid to the butter-flour mixture. Add salt, pepper, Worcestershire, shrimp, and mushrooms. Arrange the artichoke hearts in bottom of a buttered casserole (about 8 inches square). Pour shrimp sauce over artichokes. Sprinkle buttered bread crumbs on top. Bake, uncovered, in a moderately hot oven (375°) for 20 to 25 minutes, until bubbly. Makes 4 generous servings.

Shrimp Tetrazzini

Among the favorite seafood Tetrazzini recipes is this herb-flavored one made with cooked shrimp.

½ cup (¼ lb.) butter or margarine
1 cup thinly sliced green onions, including some of the tops
5 tablespoons flour
2½ cups chicken broth, canned or freshly made
½ cup clam juice
½ cup dry white wine
½ cup heavy cream
½ teaspoon oregano
½ cup shredded Parmesan cheese
2 whole cloves garlic
½ pound mushrooms, sliced
Salted water
8 ounces noodles (spaghetti or vermicelli)
4 cups deveined, cooked, shelled shrimp
Salt

Melt ¼ cup of the butter in a pan, add onions and cook, stirring, until soft. Mix in flour and gradually blend in chicken broth, clam juice, wine, cream, and oregano. Cook, stirring, for about 3 minutes after sauce begins to simmer. Stir in ¼ cup of the cheese. Set sauce aside.

Melt remaining butter in another pan, add garlic and mushrooms and cook quickly until lightly browned. Discard garlic.

Also bring to a boil a quantity of salted water, add the noodles and cook them until they are tender to bite, but not soft; then drain.

Combine sauce, mushrooms, noodles, shrimp (save a few shrimp for garnish if you like), and season with salt to taste. Pour into a large shallow casserole (9 by 13 inches) or individual casseroles. Top with shrimp and sprinkle with remaining cheese. Bake, uncovered, in a moderately hot oven (375°) until bubbling; allow 15 minutes for large casserole or 8 minutes for small ones. Broil top until lightly browned. Makes 6 to 8 servings.

Sole Baked in Wine Sauce

You don't need to worry that the fish in this dish will be dry and overcooked; the herb and wine flavored cream sauce provides fat to keep the sole moist as it is baking.

2 pounds sole fillets
2 tablespoons lemon juice
2 tablespoons dry white wine
Salt and pepper
¼ cup (⅛ lb.) butter or margarine
¼ cup flour
2 cups milk
¼ teaspoon freshly ground pepper
½ teaspoon dry mustard
1 teaspoon Worcestershire
½ teaspoon tarragon, crumbled
2 tablespoons chopped green pepper
2 tablespoons chopped parsley
2 tablespoons chopped chives
2 tablespoons grated Parmesan cheese
¼ cup sherry

Sprinkle fillets with lemon juice, wine, salt and pepper to taste; chill for several hours. Melt butter in saucepan; blend in flour until smooth. Add milk, and stirring, cook over low heat until smooth and thick. Add pepper, mustard, Worcestershire, tarragon, green pepper, parsley, chives, grated cheese, and sherry; simmer 5 minutes. Arrange fillets in a single layer in a greased baking pan (about 9 by 13 inches); pour over sauce. Bake, uncovered, in a moderate oven (350°) for 30 minutes, or until fish flakes with a fork. Makes 6 servings.

Florentined Sole *(see suggested menu below)* ✳

3 packages (10 oz. each) frozen chopped spinach
2 cups (1 pint) sour cream
3 tablespoons flour
½ cup finely chopped green onions,
    including some of the tops
Juice of 1 lemon
2 teaspoons salt
1½ to 2 pounds thin fillets of sole
2 tablespoons butter or margarine
Paprika

Cook spinach according to directions on package; drain very thoroughly. Blend sour cream with flour, green onions, lemon juice, and salt. Combine half of this mixture with spinach, and spread evenly over bottom of a shallow baking dish (about 10 by 15 inches).

Arrange sole fillets on spinach, overlapping as needed. Dot with butter. Spread remaining sour cream evenly over sole, leaving a border to show spinach, if you like. Dust lightly with paprika. (At this point you can refrigerate the dish until ready to cook.) Bake in a moderately hot oven (375°) for 25 minutes, or until fish flakes when broken with a fork. Makes 6 to 8 servings.

✳ Buffet Dinner for Six

Florentined Sole *(see recipe above)*
Parsley Potato Balls   Cucumber Salad
Hot Cheese Rolls
Raspberry Mousse with Peaches

Ideas and foods that save time are especially helpful when you entertain. This menu makes use of several shortcuts, with very good results. Assemble the fish entrée, fruit dessert, and a favorite marinated cucumber salad several hours before guests arrive. Heat frozen shredded potato balls on top of the range or in the oven, as suits you and your kitchen, and sprinkle liberally with minced parsley before serving. You can bake the rolls along with the fish.

Hot Cheese Rolls

Generously sprinkle refrigerated crescent rolls with grated American or Romano cheese before shaping; form into crescents as directed on the package and place on a greased baking sheet. Bake in a moderately hot oven (375°) for 10 to 13 minutes.

Raspberry Mousse

1 package (4¾ oz.) raspberry-currant flavored
    pudding mix
1 cup water
¼ teaspoon grated lemon peel
Juice of 1 lemon
1 package (10 oz.) frozen raspberries, thawed,
    or 1½ cups fresh raspberries and 2 tablespoons
    sugar
1 cup (½ pint) heavy cream
Sliced fresh, frozen, or canned peaches

In a saucepan blend pudding mix with water, lemon peel, lemon juice, and raspberries. Bring to a boil and cook, stirring, for 1 or 2 minutes. Chill. Whip cream and fold into raspberry mixture. Spoon into a serving bowl and chill. Decorate just before serving with sliced peaches. Pass more peaches to spoon over individual servings. Makes 6 servings.

Sole Fillets and Oysters Thermidor

Sherried mushroom sauce helps meld flavors of sole and oysters for this delectable entrée.

4 large sole fillets
1 jar (about 12 oz.) Pacific oysters
¼ pound fresh mushrooms, sliced
2 tablespoons chopped green onion (white part only)
2 tablespoons chopped green pepper
¼ cup (⅛ lb.) butter or margarine, melted
3 tablespoons flour
1 cup milk or light cream
¼ cup dry sherry
¼ cup grated Parmesan cheese
Salt and black pepper to taste
½ teaspoon dry mustard

Arrange fish fillets in a buttered baking dish (about 9 inches square), and place 2 or 3 oysters on each fillet. Sauté mushrooms, onion, and green pepper in butter; stir in flour. Gradually stir in milk or cream until blended. Add sherry, cheese, salt and pepper to taste, and mustard. Stirring, cook until smooth. Spoon sauce over fish and oysters. Bake, uncovered, in a moderate oven (350°) for 20 minutes, or until fish flakes with a fork. If desired, slip under broiler to brown lightly. Makes 4 generous servings.

French Fish Casserole

This casserole is a good choice for the cook in a hurry. The Mushroom Shrimp Sauce is a colorful topping.

1 pound sole, halibut, or haddock fillets
Water
¼ cup (4 tablespoons) vinegar
1 sprig parsley
1 small carrot, sliced
½ onion, sliced
1 teaspoon salt
¼ teaspoon pepper
1 cup canned white sauce
2 eggs, beaten

Mushroom Shrimp Sauce:
Reserved fish stock
¼ cup light cream
1 can (3 or 4 oz.) chopped mushrooms
½ cup coarsely chopped cooked shrimp
1 tablespoon cornstarch
1 tablespoon water

Cover fish with water; add vinegar, parsley, carrot, onion, salt, and pepper, and simmer for 15 minutes, or until fish flakes with a fork. Pour off stock and strain; reserve for Mushroom Shrimp Sauce. Break up fish in small pieces, then mix with white sauce and eggs. Turn mixture into a greased 1-quart casserole; place casserole in baking pan and pour ½ inch hot water in bottom of pan. Bake, uncovered, in moderate oven (350°) for 30 minutes.

Meanwhile, make Mushroom Shrimp Sauce. Cook fish stock until it is reduced to 1 cup. Add cream, mushrooms and liquid, and shrimp. Blend cornstarch with water, add to shrimp mixture, and stirring, cook until sauce is slightly thickened. Serve over hot casserole. Makes 4 to 6 servings.

Chinese Tuna Casserole

Most supermarkets now carry in cans the Chinese foods called for here: crisp chow mein noodles, chow mein vegetables, and water chestnuts.

1 can (1 lb.) chow mein vegetables
2 cans (6 or 7 oz. each) tuna
    (or a 12-oz. can)
1 small can (5 oz.) water chestnuts,
    drained and quartered
1 can (10½ oz.) cream of chicken soup
⅔ cup milk
2 teaspoons soy sauce
1 can (3 oz.) crisp chow mein noodles

In a bowl combine chow mein vegetables with tuna, water chestnuts, soup, milk, and soy sauce. Turn into lightly greased 2½-quart casserole. Cover top of casserole with crisp chow mein noodles. Bake, uncovered, in moderate oven (350°) for about 20 minutes, or until heated through. Makes 6 to 8 servings.

Tuna Cauliflower Casserole

Staples from your freezer and canned goods shelf go into this quick casserole. The baking time is just long enough to heat the cauliflower through but short enough to keep it creamy white and crunchy.

1 can (10½ oz.) mushroom soup
1 can (6 or 7 oz.) tuna, broken in small chunks
2 tablespoons chopped pimiento
1 package (10 oz.) frozen cauliflower, thawed
    slightly, separated in pieces
½ cup soft bread crumbs, mixed
    with 2 tablespoons melted butter (optional)
1 small onion, finely chopped

Spoon undiluted soup into a bowl; add tuna and pimiento; mix well, then stir in the uncooked cauliflower. Turn mixture into greased 1½-quart casserole; sprinkle with bread crumbs if desired. Bake, uncovered, in moderate oven (350°) for 20 minutes, or long enough to heat through and brown crumbs. Just before serving, sprinkle over the chopped onion. Makes 4 servings.

Tuna-Oyster Casserole

In this fondue-type casserole, the delicately flavored oysters do not lose out to the tuna. A fast broiling makes the topping crisp.

1 egg
1 cup milk
1 cup soft bread crumbs
½ teaspoon salt
Pinch of cayenne pepper
1 can (7¾ oz.) oysters, or 1 cup fresh Pacific or
    Olympia oysters
1 can (7 oz.) tuna, flaked
½ green pepper, seeded and finely chopped
1 small onion, finely chopped
¼ cup fine dry bread crumbs
2 tablespoons melted butter or margarine

Beat egg slightly, then stir in milk, soft bread crumbs, salt, and pepper. If oysters are large, cut into bite-size pieces; mix with milk mixture. Add tuna, green pepper, and onion, and mix together

well. Turn into a greased round 8-inch casserole. Toss together the dry bread crumbs and melted butter; sprinkle over top of the oyster mixture. Bake in a moderate oven (350°) for 30 minutes. Slip under the broiler for 1 minute or less to lightly brown the top. Makes 4 servings.

Herb Tuna Casserole

Additions of dill weed, celery seed, and sherry turn this otherwise familiar tuna casserole into a distinctively flavored dish.

1 can (6 or 7 oz.) tuna, drained and broken
    in pieces
1 small can (about 9 oz.) peas, drained
1 can (3 or 4 oz.) mushroom stems and pieces,
    drained (optional)
¼ teaspoon garlic salt
⅛ teaspoon dill weed
⅛ teaspoon celery seed
Dash pepper
1 can (10½ oz.) cream of mushroom soup
⅔ cup milk
2 tablespoons dry sherry
4 oz. egg noodles, cooked and drained
½ cup fresh bread crumbs, mixed with 2
    tablespoons melted butter

Butter a 1½-quart casserole and arrange drained tuna in bottom. Add drained peas (and mushrooms, if used) and season with garlic salt, dill weed, celery seed, and pepper. Combine mushroom soup, milk, and sherry; pour half of it over the first mixture. Spread noodles over top; pour remaining half of milk mixture over them. Sprinkle on bread crumbs. Bake, uncovered, in moderate oven (350°) for 30 minutes. Makes 4 servings.

Tuna-Artichoke Casserole

This rich casserole has so few ingredients that you'll want to remember it for spur-of-the-moment entertaining.

1 can (about 1 lb.) macaroni with cheese sauce
1 can (6 or 7 oz.) tuna, broken in chunks
1 can (10 oz.) marinated artichoke hearts, drained, or 1 can (1 lb.) artichoke hearts, drained
1 can (10½ oz.) white sauce
1 cup (¼ lb.) shredded sharp Cheddar cheese

Lightly grease a 2-quart casserole, then arrange macaroni with cheese sauce over bottom. Place tuna over macaroni, and arrange artichoke hearts over tuna. Spread white sauce over all. (If you use the plain rather than marinated artichoke hearts, you might like to add ⅛ teaspoon garlic powder to the white sauce.) Sprinkle with shredded cheese. Bake, uncovered, in moderate oven (350°) for 30 minutes, or until hot and bubbly and cheese browns slightly. Makes 6 servings.

Layered Tuna Casserole

If by chance or by design you have two cups of cooked rice left from a previous meal, you can quickly make this flavorful tuna casserole.

3 tablespoons butter, margarine, or bacon drippings
1 large green pepper, seeded and chopped
1 large onion, peeled and chopped
4 green onions, including tops, sliced
3 to 4 large stalks celery, sliced
1 cup chopped parsley, loosely packed
2 cups cooked rice
1 large can (9 oz.) chunk-style tuna
1 can (10½ oz.) cream of mushroom soup
¾ cup milk

Melt butter in saucepan or frying pan with tight-fitting lid. Add green pepper, onion, green onion, celery, and parsley. Cover and cook over medium heat, stirring occasionally, until vegetables are almost tender, about 6 minutes. Lightly stir in rice; turn mixture into a 2½-quart casserole.

Cover with tuna. Using the same pan, combine the soup and milk; heat to the simmering point, then pour over casserole. Bake, uncovered, in a moderate oven (400°) for about 15 minutes or until bubbly. Makes about 6 servings.

Flan de Pescado, con Aceitunas

This is a fish custard from South America, a nice dish for a luncheon or dinner.

1 small onion, sliced
2 carrot slices
1 thick lemon slice
1 teaspoon salt
Water
1 pound fillets of any white fish
½ cup stuffed green olives, chopped
½ cup light cream
6 egg yolks, beaten
Dash of pepper
½ teaspoon salt
6 egg whites
Melted butter or thin cream sauce
Minced parsley

Place onion, carrot, lemon, and 1 teaspoon salt in frying pan filled ¾ full with water. Simmer until reduced one-half, then add white fish. Simmer, covered, for 10 minutes, or until fish has lost its transparent look. Drain and chop fine.

Add olives to fish, along with cream, egg yolks, pepper, and ½ teaspoon salt. Beat egg whites until stiff and fold into mixture. Butter a 2-quart baking dish, pour in mixture, set in larger pan of hot water, and bake in moderate oven (350°) for 30 minutes, or until set. Serve with melted butter or a thin cream sauce to which minced parsley has been added. Makes 6 servings.

Asparagus spears and grated Romano cheese garnish Curry Creamed Asparagus casserole (recipe on opposite page). Serve it piping hot straight from the oven.

Vegetable Casseroles
Colorful accompaniments—easy on the cook

Artichoke Hearts in Parmesan Custard

This artichoke heart and egg casserole is superbly seasoned Italian style.

2 packages (9 oz. each) frozen artichoke hearts
½ cup canned tomatoes, drained
1 teaspoon salt
¼ teaspoon pepper
¼ teaspoon garlic salt
2 teaspoons chopped parsley
½ cup grated Parmesan cheese
¾ cup water
¼ cup olive oil
6 eggs

Arrange unthawed artichoke hearts in bottom of a greased 2-quart casserole. Cut up tomatoes over top of artichoke hearts. Sprinkle with salt and pepper, garlic salt, chopped parsley, and Parmesan cheese. Pour in water and olive oil. Cover and bake in moderate oven (350°) for 1 hour, or until artichokes are tender. Beat eggs with rotary beater until light and fluffy, pour over cooked artichokes, and continue baking, uncovered, until eggs are set, about 15 to 20 minutes longer. Makes 8 servings.

Curry Creamed Asparagus

If you want to assemble this casserole ahead of time, prepare as directed and refrigerate up to five hours before baking.

2½ pounds asparagus, washed, tough ends cut off, cut into diagonal slices about ½ inch long (reserve 3 spears for garnish)
Boiling salted water
¼ cup (⅛ lb.) butter or margarine, melted
3 tablespoons chopped green onion
¼ teaspoon curry powder
½ teaspoon salt
⅓ cup flour
2 cups milk (or 1⅔ cups milk plus ⅓ cup white wine)
⅓ cup grated Romano cheese

Lay asparagus slices and spears in a large shallow pan; pour over them enough boiling salted water to cover. Cook over high heat until water resumes boiling, reduce heat, and simmer until tender-crisp, about 8 minutes. Drain well.

Add to melted butter in a saucepan the onion, curry powder, and salt, and cook for a few minutes. Stir in flour. Gradually add milk (or milk-wine mixture); cook and stir over medium heat until mixture boils and thickens, about 10 minutes. Add drained asparagus pieces and turn into shallow baking dish (about 1½-quart size). Place the 3 spears on top for garnish. Sprinkle with cheese, and bake, uncovered, in hot oven (425°) for 15 minutes (if refrigerated, for 25 minutes). Makes 4 to 6 servings.

Asparagus Casserole

Green asparagus flecked with red pimiento and baked in a cheese custard makes this dish especially attractive.

3 eggs, well beaten
1 teaspoon salt
¼ teaspoon pepper
¾ cup cracker crumbs
1 pimiento, cut in small pieces
1 cup ¼-inch cubes of Cheddar cheese
1 cup milk
1 can (1 lb.) cut asparagus, drained,
 or 1 package (10 oz.) frozen asparagus, cooked,
 drained, cut in 2-inch pieces
3 tablespoons butter or margarine, melted

Add to the eggs, the salt, pepper, cracker crumbs, pimiento, cheese, and milk. Stir in the asparagus and pour into a greased 1½-quart casserole. Pour butter over the top. Set into a moderate oven (350°) and bake, uncovered, until the custard has set, about 30 minutes.

You can assemble this dish ahead, pouring the melted butter over the top just before baking it at mealtime. Or you can prepare and bake it ahead, and reheat it in a warm oven. Makes about 6 servings.

Asparagus in Wine

You can cook the asparagus ahead of time, then add the butter-wine sauce and the cheese topping just before you bake this tasty casserole.

2 pounds asparagus, washed, tough ends cut off
Boiling salted water
¼ cup (⅛ lb.) butter or margarine, melted
¼ cup white wine
½ teaspoon salt
¼ teaspoon pepper
⅓ cup grated Parmesan cheese

Lay asparagus spears in large shallow pan; pour over them enough boiling salted water to cover. Cook over high heat until water resumes boiling, reduce heat, and simmer until tender-crisp, about 8 minutes. Drain well and turn into a buttered 1-quart casserole.

Stir wine into melted butter. Pour butter-wine sauce over asparagus. Sprinkle with salt, pepper, and cheese. Bake, uncovered, in hot oven (425°) for 15 minutes (if refrigerated, for 25 minutes). Makes 4 to 6 servings.

Green Beans with Swiss Cheese Sauce

When you have guests for dinner, it's often convenient to serve a vegetable casserole. This one is especially delicious with roast beef or a lamb roast.

1 tablespoon butter, melted
1 tablespoon flour
½ teaspoon salt
½ teaspoon sugar
⅛ teaspoon pepper
¼ cup milk
½ teaspoon grated onion
½ cup sour cream
2 cans (1 lb. each) small whole green beans,
 drained
1½ cups shredded Swiss cheese
⅓ cup cornflake crumbs, combined
 with 1 tablespoon melted butter

In a small pan, blend thoroughly with melted butter the flour, salt, sugar, and pepper; cook, stirring, until bubbly. Blend in milk. Remove from heat and stir in onion and sour cream until well mixed. Combine sauce with green beans and cheese and turn into a buttered 1½-quart casserole. Spread buttered cornflake crumbs on top. Bake, uncovered, in hot oven (400°) for about 20 minutes. Makes 6 to 8 servings.

Company Vegetable Casserole

You can prepare this delicious casserole from ingredients that you keep on hand in the freezer and on cupboard shelves.

2 packages (10 oz.) each frozen cut green beans,
    cooked until barely tender, drained
1 can (1 lb.) bean sprouts, drained
1 can (4 oz.) water chestnuts, drained, sliced
1 can (3 or 4 oz.) mushroom pieces, drained
1 can (10½ oz.) cheese sauce
1 small onion, minced
1 can (3½ oz.) fried onion rings

Toss green beans lightly with bean sprouts, water chestnuts, and mushroom pieces. Turn into a shallow casserole (about 2-quart size). Combine cheese sauce with onion and spoon over vegetables. Bake, uncovered, in a moderate oven (350°) for 25 minutes. Top casserole with fried onion rings and bake for 10 minutes more. Makes 6 servings.

Crisp fried onion rings are the topping on this well-seasoned Green Bean Casserole (below).

Deviled Green Beans

This flavorful side dish for roasted or barbecued meat looks as good as it tastes.

1 medium-sized onion, chopped
1 clove garlic, minced
½ green pepper, chopped
2 canned pimientos, sliced or chopped
3 tablespoons butter or margarine
2 teaspoons prepared mustard
1 can (8 oz.) tomato sauce
1 cup (¼ lb.) shredded Cheddar cheese
1 package (10 oz.) frozen cut green beans,
    cooked, and drained, or 1 can (1 lb.) cut
    beans, drained

Sauté onion, garlic, green pepper, and pimientos in butter or margarine until onions are limp. Stir in mustard, tomato sauce, and cheese. Combine beans and sauce; turn into a greased 1-quart casserole. Bake, uncovered, in moderate oven (350°) for 25 minutes, or until cheese is melted. Makes 4 servings.

Green Bean Casserole

This green bean casserole, seasoned with mustard and Worcestershire and topped with fried onion rings, is a fine flavor combination for grilled ham.

3 to 4 cups cooked cut green beans (fresh,
    frozen, or canned), drained
2 tablespoons butter, melted
1½ cups milk
1 package cream of leek dry soup mix
    (amount for 3 or 4 servings)
1 tablespoon Worcestershire
½ teaspoon prepared mustard
½ cup sliced ripe olives (2¼ oz. can), drained
1 can (3½ oz.) fried onion rings or 1 cup
    coarsely crushed potato chips

Turn the cooked, drained, green beans into a greased 1½-quart casserole. Blend with melted butter the milk, dry soup mix, Worcestershire, mustard, and olives. Pour over the beans in the casserole. Then sprinkle the fried onion rings or crushed potato chips over the top.

Bake, uncovered, in a moderate oven (350°) for about 15 to 20 minutes, or until hot and bubbly. Makes about 6 servings.

Crisp-Topped Beans with Hominy

There's an unusual topping on this hearty casserole—strips of tortillas that have been browned and crisped in a pan and then combined with cheese.

1 medium-sized onion, chopped
1 clove garlic, minced or mashed
2 tablespoons butter or margarine
1 can (1 lb.) red kidney beans
1 can (1 lb.) hominy, drained
1 large can (1 lb., 13 oz.) tomatoes,
   broken up with fork
½ cup chopped green pepper
3 teaspoons chili powder
½ teaspoon salt
3 slices bacon
4 tortillas, cut in thin strips
½ cup shredded Cheddar cheese
¼ cup grated Parmesan cheese

Sauté onion and garlic in butter in large frying pan until onion is lightly browned. Add beans, hominy, tomatoes, green pepper, chili powder, and salt. Simmer, uncovered, for 15 minutes, then pour into greased 2-quart casserole.

Meanwhile in another pan, fry bacon until crisp; remove bacon and drain, leaving bacon fat in pan. Add tortilla strips to hot bacon fat and quickly toss until lightly browned and crisp, about 2 minutes.

Crumble bacon into tomato mixture along with ¼ cup of the Cheddar cheese. Sprinkle crisp tortillas over top of casserole, then sprinkle with combination of remaining Cheddar and Parmesan cheeses.

Bake, uncovered, in moderate oven (350°) for about 30 minutes, or until heated through. Makes 6 to 8 servings.

Kidney Bean and Pork Sausage Casserole

Canned kidney beans are used in this easy-to-prepare casserole, which is topped with crisp, brown pork sausage.

3 cans (about 1 lb. each) kidney beans, drained
2 medium-sized onions, chopped
2 cans (4 oz. each) sliced pimientos
¼ cup (⅛ lb.) butter or margarine, melted
½ pound bulk pork sausage
½ cup brown sugar, firmly packed
2 teaspoons salt
1 teaspoon pepper

Spoon drained kidney beans into a 2½-quart casserole; set aside. In a large frying pan, cook onions and pimientos in the melted butter over low heat until soft but not brown, about 15 minutes. Stir the onion-pimiento mixture into the beans in the casserole. In the same frying pan, brown sausage; drain off excess fat. Add to sausage the brown sugar, salt, and pepper; stir until well blended. Spread sausage mixture over the beans. Bake, uncovered, in a moderate oven (350°) for about 1 hour, or until sausage is crisp. Makes 6 to 8 servings.

Baked Beans Supreme

Pineapple and bacon give the canned pork and beans a delicious fruity and smoky taste in this casserole. Use it to accompany barbecued meats or as a main dish for supper.

½ pound sliced bacon, diced
2 medium-sized onions, chopped
2 cans (about 1 lb., 4 oz. each) pork and beans
1½ teaspoons dry mustard
1 can (9 oz.) crushed pineapple
¼ cup chili sauce
¼ teaspoon salt

Sauté bacon and onions slowly until onions are soft; drain off fat. Combine bacon and onions with beans, mustard, pineapple, chili sauce, and salt, and put into a casserole or bean pot (about 1½-quart size). Cover and bake in a very slow oven (275°) for 1½ to 2 hours. Makes 6 servings.

Hearty Bean Casserole

This dish uses three kinds of canned beans, three meats, and two wines. It's a handsome casserole to gaze upon and a husky one to eat.

1 can (1 lb.) red kidney beans
1 can (1 lb.) garbanzo beans
1 can (1 lb.) black-eyed peas
¼ teaspoon thyme
¼ teaspoon coarse-ground black pepper
1 bay leaf, crumbled fine
2 large onions, quartered
¼ pound lean pork, cut in small pieces
¼ pound lean veal, cut in small pieces
4 tablespoons olive oil
1 cup white wine
½ cup muscatel
6 little pork sausages, fried, drained, cut in small pieces

In a large bowl, mix beans and peas with thyme, pepper, and bay leaf. Place onions in 2-quart casserole. Pour bean mixture on top. Cover and bake in a very slow oven (225°) for 2 hours.

Meanwhile, brown pork and veal in olive oil. Pour white wine and muscatel over meat and simmer, covered, until beans are ready. Add sausage to other meat and stir into bean casserole. Pour over wine mixture in which meat has simmered. Add water if necessary so liquid just shows in the casserole. Cover and return to oven to bake for an additional two hours or so. Makes 6 generous servings.

Mushroom Lima Bake

Fresh mushrooms and mushroom soup are combined with baby limas in this richly flavored casserole. It is a good picnic choice because it will stay hot for several hours if wrapped in many layers of newspaper.

4 medium-sized onions, thinly sliced
½ pound fresh mushrooms, sliced
4 tablespoons butter or margarine
1 can (10½ oz.) cream of mushroom soup
1 teaspoon salt
1 teaspoon Worcestershire
½ teaspoon pepper

3 packages (10 oz. each) frozen baby limas, cooked in ¾ cup water for 5 minutes, drained
½ cup grated Parmesan cheese
½ cup heavy cream

In a frying pan, sauté onions and mushrooms in butter until vegetables are limp. Stir in cream of mushroom soup, salt, Worcestershire, and pepper. Combine parboiled limas and mushroom mixture and turn into a buttered 3-quart casserole (preferably one that has a lid if you plan to keep it hot for a picnic). Sprinkle top with Parmesan cheese, and pour over top heavy cream. Bake, uncovered, in moderate oven (350°) for 35 to 40 minutes or until casserole bubbles. Makes 8 to 10 servings.

Lima-Sausage Casserole

Serve this dish as an important accompaniment to barbecued meat, or top it with extra sausages and serve it as a luncheon or supper main dish.

4 cups fresh shelled limas or 2 packages (10 oz. each) frozen limas, thawed
1 package (8 oz.) brown-and-serve sausages, each sausage cut into 4 pieces
1 can (4 oz.) pimientos, drained, sliced
¾ teaspoon salt
¼ pound (1 cup) shredded sharp Cheddar cheese
3 tablespoons catsup
1 can (10½ oz.) white sauce
½ cup milk
½ cup fine dry bread crumbs, mixed with 2 tablespoons melted butter or margarine

Combine limas with sausage, pimientos, salt, cheese, catsup, and white sauce blended with milk; turn into a 2½-quart casserole or baking dish. Sprinkle buttered bread crumbs over the top. Bake, uncovered, in moderate oven (350°) for about 40 minutes, or until tender. Makes 6 to 8 servings.

Lima Bean and Pear Casserole (see suggested menu below) *

½ cup (¼ lb.) butter or margarine
6 cups cooked and drained lima beans (about
   1 pound uncooked dry limas), or 3 cans
   (15 oz. each) lima beans, drained
1 can (1 lb.) pears, drained and chopped
¾ cup brown sugar, firmly packed

Dot a 2½ or 3-quart casserole or bean pot with half of the butter. Cover bottom of the casserole with 2 cups beans; top with half the pears and half of the brown sugar. Repeat layers, ending with the last 2 cups of beans; distribute remaining butter over top layer. Bake in a slow oven (275°) for 2 hours. (If you want to take this dish to a picnic, cover and wrap casserole in a thick layer of newspapers to hold heat until ready to eat. It will keep warm for 3 to 4 hours.) Makes 6 to 8 servings.

---

* A Casserole Picnic

Cold Spareribs
Lima Bean and Pear Casserole (see recipe above)
Celery Sticks
Gingerbread with Sugar Glaze
Coffee   Milk

A hot bean casserole, kept warm in layers of paper, is a welcome addition to a cool-weather picnic. Cold spareribs, crisp celery sticks, and gingerbread complete the menu.

Cold Spareribs

6 pounds lean spareribs
1 bottle (12 oz.) chili sauce
2½ cups water
½ teaspoon allspice
2 teaspoons Worcestershire
2 tablespoons brown sugar
1 teaspoon salt
1 medium onion, chopped

Cut spareribs into individual ribs and place in a large baking pan, lean side up. Bake in a hot oven (400°) for 30 minutes. Drain off fat. Blend together chili sauce, water, allspice, Worcestershire, brown sugar, salt, and onion; pour over ribs. Continue cooking in a moderate oven (350°) for an additional 1 hour and 15 minutes, basting every 15 minutes. Drain ribs thoroughly on cake cooling rack and allow to cool. Refrigerate. Place in a covered container to carry to picnic site; serve as finger food with plenty of napkins. Makes 6 servings.

Gingerbread with Sugar Glaze

Make your favorite recipe of gingerbread, or use a mix and follow package directions. Frost gingerbread while it is still warm with 1 cup sifted powdered sugar blended with 1½ tablespoons milk, 1 tablespoon melted butter or margarine, and ½ teaspoon grated lemon peel. Carry to picnic in the baking pan.

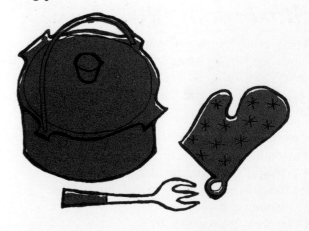

Lima Bean and Zucchini Casserole

Buttered almonds top this combination of zucchini and lima beans. The zucchini stays slightly crisp, a nice contrast to the softer limas.

1 package (10 oz.) frozen small limas
Boiling salted water
4 medium-sized zucchini, scrubbed, stemmed, cut into thin slices
1 can (3 or 4 oz.) sliced mushrooms, drained
1 can (10½ oz.) mushroom soup
¼ cup minced onion
¼ teaspoon salt
2 teaspoons chopped parsley
⅓ cup sliced almonds, mixed with 1 tablespoon melted butter

Cook the limas in small amount of boiling salted water for 5 minutes, drain, and turn into a greased 1½-quart casserole. Add zucchini to casserole with mushrooms, mushroom soup, onion, salt, and parsley; mix until blended. Cover the casserole and bake in moderate oven (350°) for 35 minutes. Remove from oven, sprinkle with almonds that have been mixed with the melted butter. Put back into oven, uncovered, and continue to bake for 15 minutes, or until the zucchini is tender but still slightly crisp. Makes about 6 servings.

Curried Lima Beans

For an enriching variation of this casserole, add two tablespoons finely chopped ham to the crumb topping.

5 pounds fresh limas in the pod, shelled (or 2 packages, 10 oz. each, frozen large limas), cooked, drained
2 tablespoons finely chopped onion
¼ cup (⅛ lb.) butter, melted
2 tablespoons flour
2 teaspoons curry powder
1½ cups milk
½ cup cracker crumbs (made from salted round butter crackers), mixed with 4 tablespoons melted butter

Turn limas into greased casserole (about 1½ quarts). Sauté onions in melted butter just until limp. Add flour and curry powder, stirring until smooth. Gradually add milk; stir until thickened. Pour sauce over beans; mix gently to coat beans. Sprinkle buttered cracker crumbs over top of beans. Bake, uncovered, in a hot oven (400°) for 15 minutes. Makes 6 servings.

Beets with Mandarin Oranges

Consider this dish when your menu calls for a brightly colored vegetable.

⅓ cup sugar
1½ teaspoons cornstarch
2 tablespoons lemon juice
⅓ cup dry white wine or liquid drained from mandarin oranges (if you use liquid from mandarin oranges, increase lemon juice to 4 tablespoons)
2 tablespoons butter or margarine
1 can (11 oz.) mandarin oranges, drained
2 cans (1 lb. each) small whole beets, drained

In a saucepan combine sugar and cornstarch. Add lemon juice and wine or orange liquid; stir until well blended. Add butter and cook over medium heat, stirring, until it boils and thickens. Remove from heat. Lightly combine drained oranges and beets in greased 1½-quart casserole. Pour over thickened sauce. Cover casserole and refrigerate until you plan to serve it. Then heat in moderate oven (350°) for about 15 minutes, or until heated through. If you prefer to serve this dish right away, combine sauce with oranges and beets in saucepan; cover and cook slowly just until heated through. Makes 6 to 8 servings.

Glazed Broccoli with Almonds

The topping that covers this broccoli casserole is crunchy with slivered almonds and crusty with toasted cheese.

2 pounds fresh broccoli, separated, or 2
    packages (10 oz. each) frozen broccoli
Boiling water
½ teaspoon salt
¼ cup (⅛ lb.) butter or margarine
¼ cup flour
1 cup light cream
1 bouillon cube, dissolved in ¾ cup hot water
2 tablespoons sherry
2 tablespoons lemon juice
Pepper to taste
½ teaspoon monosodium glutamate
¼ cup grated Parmesan cheese or ½ cup
    shredded Cheddar cheese
¼ cup slivered toasted almonds

Cook broccoli in small amount of boiling water seasoned with ½ teaspoon salt until barely tender; drain, then arrange in shallow 8 by 12-inch baking dish or casserole. While broccoli is cooking, melt butter and blend in flour. Pour in cream and bouillon cube dissolved in water; stirring, cook until smooth and thickened. Add the sherry, lemon juice, pepper, and monosodium glutamate. Pour sauce over broccoli. Sprinkle cheese and almonds over the top. Bake, uncovered, in moderately hot oven (375°) for 20 minutes, or until hot. Makes 6 servings.

Broccoli Casserole

Here's a good vegetable dish to remember when you are planning a company meal.

1 package (10 oz.) frozen chopped broccoli,
    or about 1½ pounds fresh broccoli
Salted water
2 tablespoons butter, melted
2 tablespoons flour
¼ teaspoon salt
Dash pepper
1 cup milk
1 tablespoon scraped onion
¾ cup mayonnaise
3 eggs, well beaten

Cook frozen broccoli in boiling salted water just until thawed and bright green, then drain; or trim fresh broccoli, cook until tender but still slightly crisp, then drain and coarsely chop. In another pan, blend with melted butter the flour, salt and pepper, and cook until bubbly. Gradually stir in milk, and cook, stirring, until thickened and smooth. (For a short-cut, substitute 1 can, 10½ oz., white sauce, heated, for the butter, flour, salt, pepper, and milk.) Remove from heat and stir in onion, mayonnaise, and beaten eggs. Carefully mix in the broccoli. Turn into a 2-quart casserole. Set the casserole, uncovered, in a pan of hot water. Bake in moderate oven (350°) about 30 minutes, or until the custard sauce has set. Makes 6 servings.

Easy Scalloped Carrots

If you have both leftover cooked carrots and celery, a mushroom soup sauce dresses them up for a second appearance.

2 cups cooked sliced carrots
1 cup cooked sliced celery
1 can (10½ oz.) cream of mushroom soup
⅓ cup shredded Cheddar cheese

Mix together carrots, celery, and mushroom soup in greased 1½-quart baking dish. Sprinkle the top with cheese. Bake, uncovered, in a moderately hot oven (375°) for 15 minutes, or until cheese is melted. Makes 6 servings.

Carrot and Rice Casserole *(see suggested menu below)* ✱

This flavorful carrot and rice dish is a good accompaniment for baked chicken.

½ cup uncooked regular rice
1½ cups thinly sliced carrots
¼ teaspoon powdered ginger
¼ teaspoon grated orange peel
1 tablespoon chopped parsley
1 tablespoon instant minced onion
4 teaspoons chicken stock base or 2 chicken
   bouillon cubes
1½ cups boiling water
1 tablespoon butter

Place rice in a shallow pan and lightly brown in hot oven (400°) for 8 to 10 minutes. Place browned rice in shallow, lightly buttered 1½-quart casserole; mix in the carrots, ginger, orange peel, parsley, and onion. Dissolve the chicken stock base or bouillon cubes in the boiling water; add butter. When butter is melted, pour chicken stock over the rice; cover and bake at 400° for about 25 minutes, or until liquid has been absorbed. Makes 4 servings.

✱ Baked Chicken Dinner

Tomato Juice Cocktail
Baked Chicken Paprika
Carrot and Rice Casserole *(see recipe above)*
Lemon-dressed Green Salad
Seasoned Rye Crackers
Persian Melon with Lime Sherbet

Paprika-seasoned chicken and a carrot and rice casserole bake together for this low-calorie dinner.

Tomato Juice Cocktail

Season 1 small can (1 pt., 2 oz.) tomato juice with 1 tablespoon lemon juice, ⅛ teaspoon salt, ⅛ teaspoon pepper, and ⅛ teaspoon Worcestershire. Serve chilled. Makes 4 servings.

Baked Chicken Paprika

1 broiler-fryer, cut in pieces
1 teaspoon paprika
¾ teaspoon salt
½ teaspoon sugar
⅛ teaspoon pepper

Wash chicken and pat dry with paper towels. Arrange in a single layer skin side up in a buttered baking pan; sprinkle with a mixture of the paprika, salt, sugar, and pepper. Bake in a hot oven (400°) for 35 minutes; turn pieces and cook for 10 to 15 minutes longer. Makes 4 servings.

Lemon-dressed Green Salad

Wash, drain, and separate leaves from 1 small head romaine lettuce; arrange in a salad bowl, cover, and refrigerate. Just before serving, sprinkle with 1 teaspoon sugar, ¼ teaspoon salt, and a mixture of 1 tablespoon each lemon juice and water. Toss and serve. Garnish with 4 thin slices of lemon. Makes 4 servings.

Persian Melon with Lime Sherbet

Top each of 4 wedges of chilled Persian melon with a small scoop (about ⅓ cup) of lime sherbet. Sprinkle flaked coconut or toasted flaked coconut over sherbet. Makes 4 servings.

Company Carrots

This colorful vegetable dish cooks in the oven unattended until serving time.

2 bunches (about 2½ pounds) carrots
Boiling salted water
¼ cup cooking liquid from carrots
½ cup mayonnaise
1 tablespoon minced onion or instant minced onion
1 tablespoon prepared horse-radish
Salt and pepper to taste
¼ cup fine cracker crumbs
2 tablespoons butter or margarine
Paprika and chopped parsley (optional)

Cook the whole carrots in the salted water until just tender; save ¼ cup of cooking liquid. Cut carrots lengthwise into narrow strips and arrange in shallow baking dish (8 or 9 inches square). Combine the ¼ cup liquid from cooking carrots with mayonnaise, onion, horse-radish, and salt and pepper to taste. This much can be done ahead.

Just before mealtime, pour the sauce over the carrots. Sprinkle cracker crumbs on top and dot with butter. Also sprinkle paprika and chopped parsley over top, if you wish. Bake, uncovered, in a moderately hot oven (375°) for 15 to 20 minutes. Makes about 6 servings.

Cauliflower with Cheese Sauce

Sesame seed embellishes this mixed vegetable casserole.

1 large head cauliflower (approx. 2 lbs.)
Boiling salted water
1 medium-sized onion, chopped
1 small green pepper, seeded and chopped
1 small can (2 oz.) mushroom stems and pieces
3 tablespoons butter or margarine, melted
¼ pound (1 cup) shredded sharp Cheddar cheese
2 cans (10½ oz. each) white sauce
2 tablespoons sesame seed, toasted

Separate cauliflower into flowerets and cook in boiling salted water about 10 minutes or until barely tender; drain. Sauté onion, green pepper, and mushrooms in melted butter until onion is clear. Alternate layers of cooked cauliflower, sautéed vegetables, shredded cheese, and white sauce in a greased 2-quart casserole. Sprinkle with sesame seed. Bake, uncovered, in moderate oven (350°) for 30 minutes or until bubbly. Makes 8 servings.

Cheese Cauliflower with Almond Topping

This casserole offers a particularly interesting play of textures. Be sure to use Dijon-style mustard for the special flavor it contributes.

1 large cauliflower
Boiling salted water
¼ cup (⅛ lb.) butter or margarine, melted
2 tablespoons flour
2 teaspoons chicken stock base
1 cup milk
3 ounces process Swiss Gruyère cheese
1 teaspoon Dijon-style mustard
½ cup water
¼ cup (⅛ lb.) butter
½ package (8 oz. size) herb stuffing mix
⅓ cup slivered toasted almonds

Trim whole cauliflower and cook, covered, in boiling salted water just until tender, about 25 minutes. Drain and gently separate into flowerets. Place them in greased casserole (about 2 quarts). In a saucepan, stir into the ¼ cup melted butter the flour and chicken stock base to make a smooth paste. Gradually add milk; cook, stirring, until thickened. Add cheese and mustard; continue to cook until blended and smooth. Pour sauce over cauliflower. Heat together the ½ cup water and ¼ cup butter. Pour in stuffing mix; add nuts, combine thoroughly. Spread over cauliflower. Bake, uncovered, in hot oven (400°) for 20 minutes. Makes 8 servings.

Scalloped Fresh Corn (see suggested menu below) ✱

3 cups fresh corn, cut from cob
½ cup sliced ripe olives
½ to ¾ cup diced Mozzarella cheese
¾ teaspoon salt
¼ teaspoon pepper
1½ tablespoons butter

Combine corn with olives, cheese, salt, and pepper. Pour into a shallow 1½ to 2-quart casserole. Dot with butter. Bake, uncovered, in a moderate oven (350°) for 25 minutes or until cheese is melted and bubbling. Makes 6 servings.

✱ Family Supper

Nut-crusted Ham Steak
Scalloped Fresh Corn (see recipe above)
Sliced Tomatoes
Berry Patch Pudding

A fresh corn casserole is a perfect accompaniment for the unusual broiled ham steak in this menu.

Nut-crusted Ham Steak

Generously brush a ¾-inch-thick, cooked ham steak (about 1½ pounds) with a mild-flavored honey. Broil about 5 inches below heat for 3 or 4 minutes. Turn steak, brush top side with more honey, and sprinkle with ¼ cup finely chopped, salted peanuts. Broil until nut topping is lightly toasted. Carve and serve. Makes 6 servings.

Berry Patch Pudding

4 cups cleaned whole berries of your choice
   (olallieberries, boysenberries, blackberries,
   loganberries, strawberries)
1 cup sugar (more or less to suit taste)

½ teaspoon cinnamon
¼ teaspoon nutmeg
2 tablespoons butter
1 cup flour
1 tablespoon sugar
1 teaspoon baking powder
½ teaspoon salt
1 egg
½ cup milk
2 tablespoons salad oil

Butter a 2-quart, shallow baking dish and fill with berries. Sprinkle with the 1 cup sugar, cinnamon, and nutmeg. Dot with butter. Sift flour, measure, and sift again with the 1 tablespoon sugar, baking powder, and salt. Add egg, milk, and salad oil; beat until smooth. Pour over berries. Bake in moderate oven (350°) 35 minutes. Serve warm or cold. Makes 6 to 8 servings.

Corn Casserole

Three kinds of corn go into this casserole.

1 can (1 lb.) cream-style corn
1 can (1 lb.) whole kernel corn, drained
1 cup yellow hominy, drained
1 egg, beaten
Salt to taste
2 slices process American cheese
2 slices uncooked bacon
Dash of paprika

Mix cream-style corn, whole kernel corn, and hominy together. Stir in egg and salt to taste. Place mixture in a deep, 2-quart casserole. Cut cheese and bacon into 1-inch squares. Garnish top with checkerboard arrangement of cheese and bacon squares. Sprinkle with paprika. Bake, uncovered, for 30 to 35 minutes in a moderately hot oven (375°). Makes 5 servings.

Fiesta Corn

Corn baked in an egg sauce flecked with green pepper, pimiento, and olives makes an ideal company vegetable dish.

¼ cup (⅛ lb.) butter, melted
2 cups fresh corn, cut from cob
½ cup chopped green pepper
½ cup chopped pimientos
½ cup stuffed green olives, sliced
¼ cup chopped parsley
¼ cup flour
1 teaspoon salt
1 teaspoon pepper
2 cups milk
3 eggs, slightly beaten
1 cup shredded Cheddar cheese

In a large frying pan, sauté in the butter for 2 minutes the corn, green pepper, pimientos, green olives, and parsley; cover and cook for 10 minutes. Blend in flour, salt, and pepper; gradually add milk and cook, stirring, until thickened. Gradually stir the hot vegetable mixture into beaten eggs. Blend in the cheese. Turn into a buttered 2-quart casserole. Set casserole in a pan of water and bake, uncovered, in a moderate oven (350°) about 25 minutes. Makes about 8 servings.

Eggplant Acapulco

Mushrooms and Romano cheese make this an out-of-the-ordinary eggplant dish. It's a good choice for a buffet dinner or potluck supper.

1 large eggplant
Boiling salted water
¼ cup (⅛ lb.) butter or margarine
Salt and pepper to taste
½ pound fresh mushrooms, sliced
2 cans (8 oz. each) tomato sauce
½ cup fine dry bread crumbs, mixed with ½ cup grated Romano or Parmesan cheese

Place the whole, unpeeled eggplant in enough boiling salted water to cover completely; reduce heat and simmer for 10 minutes. Drain and allow to cool enough to handle. Cut it into quarters lengthwise; peel each quarter, then cut crosswise into 1-inch pieces. Arrange layers as follows in buttered 2-quart casserole, repeating layers once: eggplant pieces, dots of butter, a sprinkling of salt and pepper, uncooked mushrooms, tomato sauce, and fine dry bread crumbs and cheese mixture. Place uncovered casserole in a moderate oven (350°) and bake for ½ hour. Serve hot. Makes 6 servings.

Swiss Eggplant

You can assemble this layered casserole several hours ahead and chill until ready to cook. The topping resembles tomato-bread pudding.

½ cup chopped onion
2 tablespoons olive oil or salad oil
1 can (6 oz.) tomato paste
1¾ cups water
2 teaspoons oregano
½ cup chopped fresh parsley
1 teaspoon salt
1 large eggplant, cut in ¼-inch-thick slices
¾ pound Swiss cheese, sliced
2¾ cups ½-inch cubes day-old French bread
1 cup shredded Parmesan cheese

Make onion-tomato sauce by combining in a saucepan the onion and oil. Cook until onion is soft. Add tomato paste, water, oregano, parsley, and salt. Simmer 5 to 10 minutes.

Coat eggplant slices with onion-tomato sauce. Arrange half the slices in bottom of a greased 9 by 13-inch pan. Cover with Swiss cheese slices and spoon half the remaining sauce over cheese. Top with remaining eggplant. Mix remainder of sauce with bread, stirring to coat well, and spoon over eggplant. Sprinkle with Parmesan cheese. Cover loosely with foil and bake in moderately hot oven (350°) for 45 minutes; remove foil and bake 30 minutes more. If desired, slip casserole under broiler for a few seconds to brown topping. Makes 6 to 8 servings.

Almond Onion Casserole is quick to make with canned onions and a sauce made by combining canned mushroom soup with cheese and sherry. Try it with grilled steak.

Scalloped Mushrooms

Assemble this mushroom casserole ahead and bake it just before mealtime.

1 pound fresh mushrooms, washed, drained, and sliced
2 cups soft French bread crumbs
½ cup (¼ lb.) butter, melted
Salt and pepper
⅓ cup dry white wine

Place about a third of the mushrooms in a buttered 1½-quart baking dish; cover with about a third of the bread crumbs, and drizzle about a third of the butter over the crumbs. Sprinkle with salt and pepper. Repeat, using another third of the mushrooms, crumbs, and butter; add salt and pepper. For the top layer, cover with remaining mushrooms; sprinkle them with salt and pepper; pour wine over all. Cover and bake in a moderately slow oven (325°) for 25 minutes. Mix remaining butter and crumbs, and spoon over mushrooms. Bake, uncovered, for 10 minutes longer, or until crumbs are toasted. Makes 8 to 10 servings.

Almond Onion Casserole

This onion casserole can be used with almost any meat, poultry, or fish as long as it is quite plainly seasoned.

2 cans (about 1 lb. each) small whole onions, drained
½ cup undiluted canned mushroom soup
½ cup shredded Swiss cheese
2 tablespoons sherry or milk
¼ cup slivered or sliced almonds
1 tablespoon butter

Place onions in a well greased 1-quart casserole. In a pan combine the mushroom soup, cheese, and sherry; heat until cheese is melted. Pour over the onions in the casserole. Either in the oven or in a small pan, heat and toast the almonds in the butter until lightly browned. Sprinkle over the top of the onions. (If you prepare the casserole ahead, put the almonds on just before heating.) Bake, uncovered, in a moderate oven (350°) for about 25 minutes, or until heated through and bubbly. Cover the dish immediately, and bring to the table. Makes about 6 servings.

Party Onions

The brown sugar, which brings out the natural sweetness of the onions, combines with the butter to give them a shiny glaze.

1 pound small onions
1 cup water
1 tablespoon brown sugar
1 teaspoon salt
¼ teaspoon paprika
Pepper to taste
2 tablespoons chopped or slivered blanched almonds, or chopped filberts
¼ cup (⅛ lb.) butter or margarine
2 tablespoons flour
1 teaspoon Worcestershire

Pour boiling water over onions, let stand a few minutes, then drain and peel. Combine the 1 cup water, brown sugar, salt, paprika, and pepper, and bring to a boil. Add onions; cover and simmer for 30 minutes, or until onions are tender. Drain off liquid and save. Place onions in greased 1½-quart casserole. Brown almonds in butter; add flour and brown lightly. Stir in the liquid left from cooking the onions, cook until slightly thickened. then add Worcestershire. Pour over onions. Cover and bake in moderately hot oven (375°) for 25 minutes. Makes 6 servings.

Stuffed Onions

3 or 4 large onions (select onions with evenly shaped, overlapping layers)
1 can (4 oz.) mushroom stems and pieces
1 can (2¼ oz.) deviled ham
3 tablespoons fine dry bread crumbs
1 egg
⅛ teaspoon nutmeg
1 tablespoon mushroom liquid
Salt to taste
3 tablespoons melted butter
¼ cup chicken broth
Minced chives

Slice off root and stem ends of onions; peel. Drop onions into boiling water to cover; simmer for 20 minutes; drain thoroughly. When cool enough to handle, make a single lengthwise cut to center of each onion. Carefully take onions apart, one layer at a time. Drain mushrooms, reserving 1 tablespoon of the liquid. Finely chop mushrooms; blend with ham, bread crumbs, egg, nutmeg, the 1 tablespoon mushroom liquid, and salt. Put a teaspoonful of mushroom mixture inside each of the large onion layers, and roll the onion layer around stuffing; it will hold without tying. (Save centers for use in other dishes.)

Place onion rolls in a small casserole; pour over them the melted butter and chicken broth. Cover and bake in a moderately hot oven (375°) for 25 minutes. (You can stuff the onions ahead and put them in the oven just in time to cook for dinner.) Sprinkle with minced chives. Makes 4 or 5 servings.

Rosemary Parsnip Casserole

Fresh rosemary snipped over parsnips gives them an intriguing flavor.

12 parsnips (about 2 pounds)
Boiling salted water
About 2 tablespoons butter
¼ teaspoon fresh or dried rosemary
2 tablespoons flour
¼ cup grated Parmesan cheese
2 cups light cream
½ cup salted round butter cracker crumbs, mixed with ¼ cup (⅛ lb.) melted butter

Peel parsnips; cook in boiling salted water until tender (about 30 minutes). Drain and cut each in half, lengthwise. Arrange half the parsnips in bottom of a greased baking dish (about 2 quarts). Dot with butter, sprinkle with half the rosemary, flour, and Parmesan; drizzle with half the cream. Repeat. Sprinkle buttered cracker crumbs over top of casserole. Bake, uncovered, in hot oven (400°) for 20 minutes. Makes 6 servings.

Company Potato Casserole

This vegetable casserole facilitates serving when you have guests. It can be prepared ahead, ready to pop into the oven thirty minutes before serving time.

6 medium-sized potatoes, peeled
1 cup (½ pint) sour cream
1 can (10½ oz.) cream of chicken soup
1 teaspoon salt
¼ teaspoon pepper
¼ teaspoon curry powder
4 hard-cooked eggs, sliced
½ cup soft bread crumbs combined with
    ½ cup shredded sharp Cheddar cheese

Cook potatoes whole in boiling salted water until tender; slice about ¼ inch thick. Combine sour cream, chicken soup, salt, pepper, and curry powder. Cover bottom of a 2-quart casserole with about one-third of the potatoes. Top with a layer of egg slices, then a layer of the cream mixture, using about one-third of each. Repeat layers to use all of the potatoes, eggs, and cream mixture. Sprinkle bread crumb-cheese mixture over top. Bake, uncovered, in moderate oven (350°) about 30 minutes, until heated through and browned on top. Makes 6 servings.

Cheese Puffed Potato Casserole

The potatoes for this dish are cooked and seasoned a day ahead. The egg whites are folded in just before the casserole is baked.

8 eggs, separated
8 cups well seasoned mashed potatoes
2 cups shredded sharp Cheddar cheese
4 teaspoons finely chopped onion
4 teaspoons finely chopped green pepper
1 teaspoon celery salt
Salt
Paprika

Beat egg yolks with mashed potatoes until well mixed. Stir in cheese, onion, green pepper, celery salt, and salt to taste. Just before you are ready to bake, beat egg whites until they form soft peaks and fold into potato mixture. Spoon lightly into 2 well-greased casseroles (about 7 by 13 inches), sprinkle with paprika and bake, uncovered, in moderately hot oven (375°) for 25 minutes. Serve from electric warming trays to keep hot. Makes 12 to 14 servings.

New Potato Casserole

Instead of using diced potatoes to make this au gratin dish, you bake small whole new potatoes in a crumb-topped cheese sauce. You can prepare the casserole early in the day and pop it in the oven to heat and brown while you put the finishing touches on the rest of the meal.

2 tablespoons finely chopped onion
5 tablespoons butter or margarine
3 tablespoons flour
1 teaspoon salt
¼ teaspoon paprika
1½ cups milk
1 cup (¼ lb.) shredded Cheddar cheese
½ cup sliced ripe olives (optional)
12 small cooked and peeled new potatoes
    (about 2 lbs.)
1 cup soft bread crumbs

Sauté onion in 3 tablespoons of the butter until golden. Stir in flour, salt, and paprika. When bubbly, pour in milk; cook, stirring constantly, until mixture is smooth and thickened. Remove from heat; blend in cheese; add olives if desired. Place cooked potatoes in buttered 1½-quart casserole; pour over cheese sauce. Melt remaining 2 tablespoons butter; mix with bread crumbs. Top potatoes and sauce with buttered crumbs. Bake, uncovered, in a moderate oven (350°) for 20 to 25 minutes, until heated through and golden brown. Makes 6 servings.

Sweet Potatoes with Apricots

This sweet potato dish is quick to prepare, for the main ingredients come from cans. If you refrigerate it, allow 10 to 15 minutes additional baking time.

2 large cans (1 lb., 10 oz. each) sweet potatoes, drained, sliced
1 can (1 lb.) apricot halves, drained
½ cup brown sugar, firmly packed
¼ cup pecan halves
3 tablespoons butter, melted
1 teaspoon grated orange peel
2 teaspoons orange juice

Layer half the potatoes and half the apricots in a greased 8-inch square baking dish. Sprinkle with half the brown sugar. Repeat the layers, using the remaining potatoes, apricots, and brown sugar; top with pecans. Combine the melted butter, orange peel, and orange juice; pour over the potatoes and apricots. Bake, uncovered, in a moderate oven (350°) for 30 minutes, basting occasionally with the juices in the dish. Makes 6 servings.

Sweet Potatoes with Apple Sauce Nut Topping

During baking, the flavor of the apple sauce permeates these sweet potatoes. The sauce itself practically disappears.

2 cans (1 lb. each) sweet potatoes, drained
1 can (1 lb.) apple sauce
½ cup dark brown sugar
1 tablespoon lemon juice
½ teaspoon mace
¼ cup (⅛ lb.) butter or margarine
½ cup coarsely broken walnuts

Arrange sweet potatoes in 9-inch square baking pan or other casserole. Mix together apple sauce, brown sugar, lemon juice, and mace, and spoon over the potatoes. Dot with butter and sprinkle with nut meats. Bake, uncovered, in a moderately hot oven (375°) for 35 minutes, or until heated through. Makes 6 to 8 servings.

Oranges combine with raisins and caraway to give unusual flavor to canned sauerkraut.

Orange Sauerkraut

This tangy combination of sauerkraut with raisins and oranges is delicious with oven roast duck. Consider it also when you are having pork chops, frankfurters, lamb, or wild game.

1 large can (1 lb., 12 oz.) sauerkraut, drained
2 teaspoons grated orange peel
1 teaspoon caraway seed
½ cup raisins
½ cup orange juice
Salt and pepper to taste
2 whole oranges
2 tablespoons melted butter

Combine sauerkraut with orange peel, caraway seed, raisins, and orange juice. Add salt and pepper to taste, depending on saltiness of sauerkraut. Turn into greased 1½-quart casserole. Cover and bake in moderate oven (350°) for 1 hour. Meanwhile, peel oranges, cutting off all the white membrane; carefully lift out orange sections and remove seeds. After casserole has cooked an hour, arrange orange pieces on top and drizzle with melted butter. Return (uncovered) to the oven for about 10 minutes, or until heated through. Makes about 6 servings.

Spinach Supreme

Here is a dressed-up speedy version of creamed spinach, with sesame seed and almonds supplying a novel texture. Since this dish is baked, it doesn't have the watery quality usually associated with spinach.

2 packages (10 oz. each) frozen chopped
    spinach, or 1½ pounds fresh spinach,
    washed and finely chopped
Boiling salted water
1 can (10½ oz.) cream of mushroom soup,
    undiluted
Salt and pepper to taste
Dash of garlic salt
2 tablespoons sesame seed
Pinch of thyme (optional)
¼ cup sliced almonds

Cook frozen or fresh spinach in small amount of boiling salted water just until tender, about 5 minutes; drain very thoroughly. Mix in the mushroom soup, salt and pepper to taste, garlic salt, sesame seed, thyme if desired, and half the sliced nut meats. Turn into a buttered 1-quart casserole, and sprinkle remaining nut meats on top. Bake, uncovered, in moderate oven (350°) for 20 minutes, or until bubbly and nuts are golden brown. Makes 4 servings.

Spinach Bake

Chopped spinach mixed with egg and cheese bakes under a crusty topping of crumbled cooked bacon and fine bread crumbs.

3 slices bacon, cut in small pieces
1 small onion, minced
2 cups chopped uncooked spinach (approx. 1 lb.),
    or 2 packages (10 oz. each) frozen chopped
    spinach
1 cup shredded Cheddar cheese
2 eggs
½ teaspoon salt
Dash of pepper
3 tablespoons fine dry bread crumbs

Cook bacon until lightly browned; drain on paper towels. Pour off all but 2 tablespoons bacon drippings, add onion and cook until limp. Combine chopped spinach, cheese, and cooked onion.

Beat eggs with the salt and pepper and stir into spinach mixture. Turn into shallow, greased, 1-quart baking dish. Sprinkle with bread crumbs and bacon pieces. Bake, uncovered, in moderate oven for 40 minutes, or until spinach mixture is set. Makes 6 servings.

Spinach in Sour Cream Sauce

Just two ingredients, onion soup mix and sour cream, season the sauce.

3 packages (10 oz. each) frozen chopped spinach
Boiling salted water
½ pint (1 cup) sour cream
1 package onion soup mix (amount for 3 or
    4 servings)
½ teaspoon salt
Nutmeg if desired

Cook spinach in boiling salted water until tender; drain thoroughly. Turn into a blender the sour cream, soup mix, and salt, and blend until smooth (or beat with a mixer until well blended). Mix together the cooked spinach and sour cream mixture, and turn into a greased 1½-quart casserole. Sprinkle lightly on top with nutmeg if desired. Bake, uncovered, in moderately slow oven (325°) for 20 minutes, or until hot throughout. Makes 6 to 8 servings.

Spinach-Cheese Bake

The dark green color of spinach is prominent in this dish, yet the flavor is mild.

3 cups chopped cooked spinach (2 packages, 10 oz. each, frozen chopped spinach)
¼ pound (1 cup) shredded sharp Cheddar cheese
1 cup cooked rice
1 teaspoon salt
2 tablespoons catsup
2 tablespoons prepared horse-radish
1 tablespoon melted butter or margarine
2 hard-cooked eggs, sliced

Mix together the spinach, cheese, rice, salt, catsup, horse-radish, and melted butter. Turn mixture into greased 9 by 5-inch loaf pan. Bake in moderately slow oven (325°) for 20 minutes, or until cheese melts. Turn out on platter and garnish with slices of hard-cooked eggs. Serve with tomato sauce if desired. Makes 6 servings.

Zucchini-Rice Casserole

A vegetable plus rice in a casserole is a good way to simplify menus. This unusual combination goes well with grilled chicken or spareribs.

About 1½ pounds tender, small zucchini, sliced ¼ inch thick
¾ cup shredded sharp Cheddar cheese
½ cup regular long grain rice, uncooked
1 can (10½ oz.) mushroom soup
1 cup water
1 small can (3 or 4 oz.) sliced mushrooms
1 teaspoon salt
¼ teaspoon pepper
1 or 2 slices bacon, cut in 1-inch pieces

Arrange about a third of the zucchini in the bottom of a well buttered 2-quart casserole. Top with about one third of the cheese and half the rice. Make another layer of a third of the cheese and a third of the zucchini, then a layer using all the remaining rice. Arrange the rest of zucchini on top. In a small pan, combine the soup, water, mushrooms (including their liquid), salt, and pepper; heat and pour into the casserole. Sprinkle remaining cheese on top. Arrange bacon pieces on top. Cover and bake in moderate oven (350°) for about 25 minutes. Uncover and bake about 20 minutes longer, or until rice is tender and zucchini is tender-crisp. Makes 4 to 6 servings.

Baked Ratatouille

Ratatouille is a French vegetable stew from the southern coast that can be cooked by several methods; in this instance the vegetables are baked. You add no liquid; in fact, you may want to remove the casserole cover during baking to let the juices cook down. Serve ratatouille hot, cold, or reheated. Flavor is best if you let ratatouille stand awhile before serving.

2 large onions, sliced
2 large cloves garlic, minced or mashed
1 medium-sized eggplant, cut in ½-inch cubes
6 medium-sized zucchini, thickly sliced
2 green or red Bell peppers, seeded and cut in chunks
4 large tomatoes, cut in chunks
About 2 teaspoons salt
1 teaspoon basil
½ cup minced parsley
4 tablespoons olive oil
Parsley
Sliced tomato (optional)

Layer the onions, garlic, eggplant, zucchini, peppers, and tomatoes into a 5 to 6-quart casserole, sprinkling a little of the salt, basil, and parsley between each layer (using all of these seasonings). Press vegetables down, if necessary, to make them fit into casserole. Drizzle top layer with the olive oil. Cover casserole and bake in a moderate oven (350°) for 3 hours. Baste top occasionally with some of the liquid.

Uncover during last hour of cooking if ratatouille is quite soupy. Remove from oven, mix gently, and add salt to taste. Serve hot, or cover and chill to serve cold or reheat. Garnish with parsley sprigs and tomato slices. Makes 8 to 10 servings.

Zucchini-Corn Casserole

Mix tender-crisp zucchini with canned corn for this guest buffet casserole. To make this dish for a family dinner, you might want to cut the amounts in half and cut baking time to about 30 minutes.

3 pounds small zucchini, scrubbed, stemmed
Boiling salted water
1 can (1 lb.) cream style corn
4 eggs, slightly beaten
1 medium-sized onion, chopped
1 small green pepper, seeded and chopped
2 tablespoons butter or margarine, melted
1¼ teaspoons salt
¼ teaspoon pepper
1 cup shredded sharp Cheddar cheese
Paprika

Cook zucchini in boiling salted water until just tender, about 6 minutes. Drain squash, cut in chunks, and combine with the corn and eggs. Meanwhile, sauté onion and green pepper in butter until golden brown, about 5 minutes; add to the other vegetables with the salt and pepper. Turn into greased 2-quart casserole or baking dish. Sprinkle cheese on top, then sprinkle with paprika. Bake, uncovered, in moderate oven (350°) for about 40 minutes (30 minutes if you make the recipe in a smaller amount), or until lightly browned and bubbly. Makes 8 to 10 servings.

Zucchini Custard Casserole

The pieces of zucchini in this casserole are surrounded by a well seasoned, golden custard.

¼ cup (⅛ lb.) butter or margarine, melted
2 pounds zucchini, cut in small pieces
3 eggs
½ cup undiluted evaporated milk or light cream
2 tablespoons fine dry bread crumbs
1 teaspoon instant minced onion
1 teaspoon Worcestershire
Dash of liquid hot pepper seasoning
¾ teaspoon salt
⅛ teaspoon pepper
⅓ cup shredded Parmesan cheese

In a large frying pan that has a tight-fitting lid, add to the melted butter the zucchini pieces. Cover and cook over low heat, stirring occasionally, until tender (5 to 7 minutes). Remove from heat and set aside. Beat the eggs with the milk or cream; stir in the bread crumbs, onion, Worcestershire, hot pepper seasoning, salt, pepper, and about 2 tablespoons of the Parmesan. Combine with the zucchini, stirring until blended. Turn into a buttered 1½-quart casserole. Sprinkle the remaining cheese over top. Bake, uncovered, in a moderate oven (350°) for 35 to 40 minutes. If the dish has been refrigerated, allow about 10 minutes longer baking time. Makes 4 to 6 servings.

Green and Gold Squash

Two plentiful summer squashes are combined in this vegetable casserole. It is an ideal dish for "barbecue night," because once in the oven, it needs no tending.

1 medium-sized onion, chopped
2 tablespoons salad oil
About ¾ pound (2 or 3 medium-sized) zucchini, scrubbed, stemmed, shredded coarsely
About ¾ pound (2 medium-sized) yellow summer squash, scrubbed, stemmed, shredded coarsely
2 tablespoons chopped parsley
½ teaspoon salt
½ teaspoon oregano
¼ teaspoon pepper
3 eggs, slightly beaten
½ cup milk
1 cup shredded sharp Cheddar cheese
½ cup saltine cracker crumbs

In a large frying pan, sauté onion in salad oil until golden brown. Remove from heat; stir in shredded squash, parsley, salt, oregano, pepper, and slightly beaten eggs blended with milk. Spoon about half the mixture into a buttered 1½-quart baking dish; sprinkle with half the cheese and half the crumbs. Make a second layer of the remaining squash; sprinkle with remaining cracker crumbs. Arrange the last of the cheese in a criss-cross design on top. Bake, uncovered, in moderately slow oven (325°) for about 45 minutes. Makes 6 servings.

Cheese, macaroni, and sausage combine to make the spicy Mexican dish "Macarron con Chorizo" (page 81). Serve it as a main course, with a green salad and a fruit dessert.

Rice, Macaroni, Noodles

Versatile dishes, full flavored and hearty

Cheese Almond Rice

Here's a colorful rice dish to serve with meat that is cooked over charcoal. If you choose a heavy casserole with a tight-fitting lid, it will help keep the rice warm for serving outside.

1 can (6 or 8 oz.) sliced mushrooms, drained, liquid reserved
2 teaspoons instant chopped or minced onions
⅓ cup chopped or sliced almonds
¼ pound (1 cup) shredded Cheddar cheese
1¼ cups regular long grain rice, uncooked
⅛ teaspoon pepper
Water
3 beef bouillon cubes
4 teaspoons soy sauce
2 tablespoons chopped parsley
2 tablespoons chopped pimiento
Salt to taste

Combine drained mushrooms with onions, almonds, cheese, uncooked rice, and pepper; turn into a greased 2-quart casserole. Add water to the liquid from mushrooms to make 3½ cups liquid; heat to the simmering point. Add the bouillon cubes and soy sauce to the hot liquid and stir until bouillon cubes are dissolved. Pour over ingredients in the casserole. Cover and bake in moderately hot oven (375°) for 45 minutes to 1 hour, or until liquid has been absorbed. Stir in the parsley and pimiento just before serving. Add salt to taste, if needed. Makes 6 to 8 servings.

Chinese Rice Casserole

Spices and salt from soup mix and sausage season this dish. It is easy to double the ingredients to serve 16 or to store in your freezer. Freeze unbaked; baking time, if frozen, is about two hours.

2 packages (amount for 3 or 4 servings each) dehydrated chicken noodle soup
3 cups boiling water
1 pound pork sausage meat
2 cups finely cut celery
1 large onion, finely chopped
½ green pepper, finely cut
½ cup uncooked rice
1 small can (2 oz.) pimiento
½ can (6 oz. size) water chestnuts, drained and sliced in rounds (optional)

Put soup mixture in a large casserole (3-quart); pour over the boiling water and let stand while preparing the rest of the ingredients. Cook sausage until all the redness has gone; drain, reserving about 2 tablespoons of the drippings in frying pan. Sauté celery, onion, and green pepper in drippings until a light yellow color. Combine all the ingredients in the casserole; mix well. Cover and bake in a moderate oven (350°) about 1½ hours, stirring once after 30 minutes. If more liquid is needed, add chicken consommé. Makes 8 servings.

Rice and Chili-Cheese Casserole

This hearty casserole is especially tasty with toasted tortillas and avocado salad.

1 large onion, finely chopped
2 tablespoons butter or margarine
1 large can (1 lb., 13 oz.) tomatoes, drained
1 can (4 oz.) peeled green chilies, diced
Salt to taste
1 tablespoon flour
1 tablespoon butter or margarine, melted
1 cup light cream
1½ cups rice, boiled or steamed until tender
½ pound jack cheese, sliced

Sauté onion in the 2 tablespoons butter until lightly browned. Add tomatoes and chilies. Season with salt, and cool. For the sauce, stir flour into the 1 tablespoon melted butter; gradually add cream and cook, stirring until thickened. Cool and combine with the tomato mixture. Add cooked rice. Mix together lightly and pour into a greased 3-quart casserole. Top with sliced cheese. Bake, uncovered, in a moderate oven (350°) until heated through and cheese melts. Makes 8 servings.

Confetti Rice

By simply stirring chopped raw vegetables and almonds into rice pilaf ten minutes before it is done, you create this unusual dish.

¼ cup (⅛ lb.) butter or margarine, melted
1¼ cups long grain rice, uncooked
2 cans (10½ oz. each) consommé
½ teaspoon salt
¾ cup chopped green onions
¾ cup chopped carrots
¾ cup chopped celery
¼ cup sliced almonds

In a large frying pan, add the rice to the melted butter and cook, stirring occasionally, until heated but not browned (about 5 minutes). Add consommé and salt and continue cooking until mixture comes to a boil; turn into a 1½-quart casserole. Bake, covered, in moderately hot oven (375°) for about 30 minutes, or until rice is tender.

About 10 minutes before rice is done, remove from oven and stir in chopped raw vegetables and almonds. Return to oven and continue baking with cover on for remaining 10 minutes. The vegetables should remain quite crisp to contrast with the tender grains of rice. Makes 6 servings.

Hungarian Rice

This casserole is recommended for a picnic. By wrapping it snugly in several layers of newspaper and carrying it in an insulated bag, it will stay hot for four or five hours.

4 cups finely chopped cabbage
1 tablespoon salt
6 tablespoons butter or margarine
1 tablespoon sugar
1 cup raisins
1 cup rice
1½ cups boiling chicken stock
2 eggs, beaten
¾ cup light cream
1 teaspoon paprika (Hungarian, if available)
Salt and pepper to taste

Sprinkle cabbage with salt and let stand about 20 minutes. Squeeze out liquid. Sauté cabbage until golden in butter or margarine along with sugar and raisins, stirring occasionally. Meanwhile, add rice to boiling chicken stock. Cover, and cook slowly until liquid is absorbed. Combine with cabbage mixture, eggs, cream, paprika, and salt and pepper to taste. Pour into a 2-quart casserole; cover and bake in a slow oven (300°) for 30 minutes. Makes 5 or 6 servings.

Sopa de Arroz con Chorizo

Avocado and egg slices garnish this colorful casserole. It makes a substantial main dish.

1 pound chorizo (Mexican sausage)
¼ cup lard or shortening
2 cups uncooked rice
¼ cup minced onion
⅓ cup tomato purée
2 cups raw peas
4 cups beef stock
Salt to taste
2 hard-cooked eggs
1 large avocado

Skin chorizo and brown in lard. Mash with a fork; remove and reserve. Brown rice and onion in the same fat. Combine chorizo, tomato purée, peas, and stock and turn into a greased 2½-quart casserole. Cover and bake in a moderate oven (350°) for about 50 minutes or until rice is fluffy. Add more stock if needed; add salt to taste. Just before serving, garnish with slices of egg and avocado. Makes 6 servings.

In Mexico this casserole-type rice and chorizo dish is called a "sopa seca," or "dry soup."

Cover and bake in a moderate oven (350°) for 30 minutes; remove cover and continue baking 15 minutes to brown the top. Makes 6 to 8 servings.

Creole Casserole

Sausage extends a small amount of ham in this substantial rice dish.

1 cup uncooked rice
1 pound small link sausages
2 tablespoons sausage drippings
2 medium-sized onions, chopped
1 can (8 oz.) tomato sauce
2 green peppers, seeded and chopped
4 green onions and tops, sliced
1 cup of ½-inch cooked ham cubes
⅛ teaspoon pepper

Cook rice by any preferred method. Cut sausages into 1-inch lengths and brown lightly; remove from pan and pour off all but 2 tablespoons of the drippings. Sauté the chopped onions in drippings until limp and golden. Stir in the tomato sauce, green peppers, green onions and tops, ham cubes, and browned sausage pieces. Cook over low heat, stirring frequently for 15 minutes.

Combine the cooked rice and meat mixture in a greased 2-quart casserole; season with pepper.

Macarrón con Chorizo

Spicy Mexican sausage flavors the macaroni in this hearty main-dish casserole.

1 pound large tube-shaped macaroni
Boiling salted water
1 pound chorizo (Mexican sausage)
2 tablespoons lard or shortening
½ cup minced onion
3 cans (8 oz. each) tomato sauce
2 tablespoons chopped cilantro (Chinese parsley), or 1 teaspoon oregano
Salt and pepper to taste
6 ounces jack cheese, shredded (about 3 cups)

Boil macaroni in the boiling salted water until just tender; drain and reserve. Skin chorizo and sauté in the lard until done. Remove, break into pieces, and reserve. Cook onion in fat remaining in the pan. Add tomato sauce, cilantro, salt, and pepper. Arrange in a greased 2½-quart casserole in layers: macaroni, chorizo, sauce, and cheese. Cover and bake in a moderate oven (350°) for 30 minutes. Makes 6 servings.

Sausage and Macaroni Casserole (see suggested menu below) *

You can keep the ingredients for this attractive casserole on hand indefinitely, ready to whip together in a very few minutes.

1 can (about 1 lb.) macaroni in cheese sauce
1 package (10 oz.) frozen green beans,
  cooked and drained
1 teaspoon prepared mustard
1 can (4 oz.) Vienna sausages, drained
2 tablespoons grated Parmesan cheese

Spoon macaroni and cheese around the edge of a shallow 8-inch casserole (or pie pan). Mix beans with mustard and place in center of macaroni. Arrange sausages on macaroni; sprinkle with grated cheese. Bake, uncovered, in moderate oven (350°) for 15 minutes or until thoroughly heated. Makes 2 or 3 servings.

---

* Quick Family Supper

Sausage and Macaroni Casserole
(see recipe above)
Pickled Mushrooms with Tomatoes
Bread Sticks
Quick Apple Crisp

Here's a family casserole supper that can be whipped together in a very few minutes. The dessert can bake as you eat supper, or can be served cold.

Pickled Mushrooms with Tomatoes

Combine 1 jar (3½ oz.) whole pickled mushrooms and oil with 2 large peeled tomatoes, cut in slender wedges, and 1 or 2 tablespoons red wine vinegar. Chill and serve. Makes 3 servings.

Quick Apple Crisp

1 can (about 1 lb.) apple sauce, or 1½ cups
  canned or freshly-made apple sauce (sweetened)
Nutmeg
¼ cup raisins
⅔ cup crushed zwieback crumbs
3 tablespoons butter or margarine

Pour apple sauce into a shallow greased baking pan. Dust top lightly with nutmeg. Sprinkle with raisins and zwieback crumbs. Dot crumbs with butter. Bake in a moderately hot oven (375°) for 20 minutes. Makes 3 or 4 servings.

Glorified Macaroni and Cheese

It is a good idea to have in your recipe repertory a casserole that can be rapidly put together from canned foods, especially when the resulting dish is as elegant as this one.

2 cans (15¼ oz. each) macaroni and cheese
4 hard-cooked eggs, sliced
2 cans (10½ oz. each) green asparagus tips,
  drained, liquid reserved
1 can (4 oz.) chopped ripe olives, drained
½ cup shredded Cheddar cheese
¼ cup saltine cracker crumbs

Turn one can of the macaroni and cheese into a buttered 1½-quart casserole. Arrange 2 of the hard-cooked eggs in a layer over the macaroni. Arrange asparagus over the egg slices. Repeat these three layers, using the remaining macaroni, eggs, and asparagus. Add the olives, mixing them lightly into top layer with a fork. Pour asparagus liquid (you should have about 1 cup) over the mixture in the casserole. Combine cheese and crackers and sprinkle over the top. Bake, uncovered, in a hot oven (400°) for 25 minutes. Makes 6 to 8 servings.

Noodles with Cheese-Meat Sauce

Here's a hearty casserole that combines several kinds of cheese, a meat sauce, and noodles.

1 package (8 oz.) wide egg noodles
Boiling salted water
1 pound ground beef
1 clove garlic, minced or mashed
½ teaspoon salt
2 cans (8 oz. each) Spanish style tomato sauce
1 small package (3 oz.) cream cheese
½ pint (1 cup) sour cream
3 tablespoons cottage cheese
6 green onions and tops, finely sliced
½ cup shredded Cheddar cheese

Cook noodles in boiling salted water until tender; drain. Meanwhile, brown meat, stirring with a fork until crumbly; stir in garlic and salt. Add tomato sauce and simmer over low heat. Mix together cream cheese, sour cream, cottage cheese, and green onions. Arrange alternate layers of noodles, meat sauce, and cream cheese mixture in a 2½-quart casserole. Sprinkle top with Cheddar cheese. Bake in a moderate oven (350°) for 20 minutes. Makes 6 servings.

Noodles Romanoff

In this ideal accompaniment for barbecued meat, the sour cream really asserts itself and gives the noodles character.

1 package (8 oz.) egg noodles
Boiling salted water
1 cup large curd cottage cheese
1 small clove garlic, minced or mashed
1 teaspoon Worcestershire
1 cup (½ pint) sour cream
¼ cup grated onion
¼ teaspoon liquid hot-pepper seasoning
½ cup grated Parmesan cheese

Cook noodles in boiling salted water until just tender; drain. Combine noodles with cottage cheese, garlic, Worcestershire, sour cream, onion, and liquid hot-pepper seasoning. Turn into a buttered casserole; sprinkle grated cheese over the top. Bake, uncovered, in a moderate oven (350°)

for 25 minutes, or until heated through. Makes 8 servings.

California Casserole

Asparagus is combined with a rich mixture of other ingredients in this casserole. You can cut back on either the cheese or the almonds and still have a very satisfying dish.

1 cup broken spaghetti, uncooked
Boiling salted water
1 cup thick cream sauce
1 cup shredded mild Cheddar cheese
⅛ teaspoon dry mustard
⅛ teaspoon paprika
½ cup dry white wine
1 cup cooked asparagus tips
1 pound fresh crab meat
½ cup chopped toasted almonds

Break spaghetti into 2-inch pieces; cook in boiling salted water until barely tender. Heat cream sauce and add cheese, mustard, and paprika. When cheese is melted, stir in wine. Cover the bottom of a greased 1-quart casserole with a little of the sauce. Add half the cooked spaghetti in a thin layer, then a layer of asparagus and a layer of crab. Cover with about half the remaining sauce and add a few chopped almonds. Then repeat layers of spaghetti, asparagus, and crab; pour on remaining sauce; and top with remaining almonds. Set casserole in a shallow pan of hot water. Place in moderately slow oven (325°) and bake, uncovered, approximately 30 minutes or until hot and bubbling. Makes 4 to 6 servings.

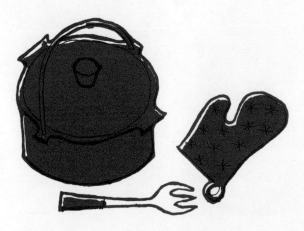

Eggs and Cheese

Casserole favorites for brunch or supper

Ham and Egg Casserole

Ham and eggs have long been a standard breakfast dish; try them "en casserole" for a brunch menu, along with hot buttered biscuits and marmalade.

5 tablespoons butter or margarine
4 tablespoons flour
2 cups milk
½ teaspoon salt
⅛ teaspoon chervil (optional)
Dash pepper
6 hard-cooked eggs, sliced in ¼-inch
   crosswise slices
1 cup cubed cooked ham
1 can (6 or 8 oz.) chopped or sliced
   mushrooms, drained
1 cup crushed cornflakes or cornflake crumbs

Melt 3 tablespoons of the butter in a small pan over medium heat. Stir in the flour and when smooth, gradually stir in the milk. Cook, stirring, until the mixture thickens. Stir in the salt, chervil (if used), and pepper. In a greased 2-quart casserole, arrange alternate layers of the hard-cooked egg slices, ham cubes, and mushrooms. Pour the thickened sauce over the top.

Melt the remaining 2 tablespoons butter in a small pan and mix in the cornflake crumbs; then sprinkle on top of the casserole. Bake, uncovered, in a moderate oven (350°) for about 25 minutes or until top is golden.

Deviled Egg-Shrimp Casserole

Here are deviled eggs served in a bubbling cheese and shrimp sauce. Since this dressy dish lacks the starchy base of many casseroles, it will appeal especially to women.

¼ cup (⅛ lb.) butter or margarine, melted
¼ cup flour
½ teaspoon salt
2 cups milk
1½ cups shredded sharp Cheddar cheese
   (about 6 oz.)
½ teaspoon Worcestershire
¼ teaspoon dry mustard
1 teaspoon grated onion
6 hard-cooked eggs, deviled
¾ pound cleaned, cooked shrimp, or 2 cans
   (5 oz. each) shrimp
½ cup soft bread crumbs mixed with 2
   tablespoons melted butter

Stir into melted butter the flour and salt. Add milk gradually, stirring until smooth. Reduce heat; add cheese and stir until melted. Add Worcestershire, mustard, and onion. Arrange deviled eggs in greased 9-inch-square baking pan. Sprinkle with shrimp. Pour over cheese sauce, and top with crumbs. Bake, uncovered, in moderate oven (350°) for 25 minutes, or until bubbly. Makes 6 servings.

For an attractive and easy-to-prepare brunch dish, serve Tomatoes and Eggs Italian (page 86)—eggs poached in a mixture of fresh tomatoes and mushrooms. Figs, Italian ham, toast, and coffee complete the menu.

Tomatoes and Eggs Italian

This quick casserole is made by poaching eggs in a fresh tomato and mushroom mixture.

1 pound mushrooms, sliced
3 tablespoons butter or margarine
3 or 4 large tomatoes, peeled, cut in cubes, drained
6 or 8 eggs
Salt and pepper
¾ cup shredded cheese

Sauté mushrooms in 3 tablespoons butter or margarine until cooked. Set aside a few mushroom slices for garnish. Add tomatoes and stir to heat through. With a spoon, make 6 or 8 nest spaces and break an egg in each space. Season with salt and pepper, top with shredded cheese, and garnish with mushroom slices. Cover pan and cook until eggs are set. Makes 3 or 4 servings.

Baked Ham and Eggs

You can prepare this casserole ahead of time, to the point of adding eggs.

1 large onion, sliced
¼ pound ham, diced
3 tablespoons butter or margarine
1 clove garlic, minced or mashed
3 medium-sized tomatoes, peeled and chopped
1 to 1½ cups cooked peas, beans, carrots, corn, or a combination of vegetables
1 tablespoon finely chopped parsley
¼ teaspoon salt
⅛ teaspoon pepper
½ cup sliced pimiento-stuffed green olives
8 eggs
½ cup shredded Swiss or Cheddar cheese

In frying pan, cook onion and ham in melted butter over medium heat, stirring, until onion is tender (about 5 minutes). Add garlic and tomatoes; cook slowly for about 10 minutes. Add vegetables, parsley, salt, pepper, and olives. Turn into 8 baking dishes (about 10-ounce size).

Break the eggs; carefully slip one into each dish. Sprinkle cheese on top. Bake, uncovered, in moderate oven (350°) for about 20 minutes, or until eggs are to your liking. If you prefer, you can bake this in an 8-inch square dish, for about the same length of time. Serve each egg with some of the sauce on crisp toast. Makes 8 servings.

Curried Eggs with Shrimp Sauce

Curry-flavored eggs are given a shrimp sauce topping in this baked supper dish.

8 hard-cooked eggs
1 teaspoon salt
Dash of Worcestershire
½ teaspoon curry powder
½ teaspoon paprika
¼ teaspoon dry mustard
Juice of ½ lemon (1½ tablespoons)
2 to 3 tablespoons sour cream

Cheese-Shrimp Sauce:
2 cups milk or light cream
2 tablespoons butter or margarine
2 tablespoons flour
1 teaspoon salt
Pepper to taste
1 teaspoon Worcestershire
1 cup shredded sharp Cheddar cheese
2 cans (5 oz. each) shrimp

Cut eggs in half lengthwise and scoop out yolks. Mash egg yolks with salt, Worcestershire, curry powder, paprika, mustard, and lemon juice; moisten with sour cream. Fill egg halves with mashed yolks and press together. Place in a greased baking dish (8 or 9 inches square).

For the sauce, heat milk to scalding point. Make a roux with the butter and flour and blend in; stirring constantly, cook until smooth and thick. Add salt, pepper, Worcestershire, and cheese, and heat until melted. Stir in shrimp. Pour sauce over the deviled eggs. Bake, uncovered, in moderate oven (350°) for 20 minutes. Makes 4 to 6 servings.

Egg and Rice Casserole

This rich egg and rice casserole goes well with croissants or English muffins and your favorite breakfast meat. You can assemble the casserole the night before a brunch, and bake it just before serving. (Add 10 to 15 minutes to the total baking time if it is cold from the refrigerator.)

1 medium-sized onion, chopped
2 cups uncooked regular rice
6 tablespoons butter or margarine
5½ cups chicken stock (fresh, canned, or
    made from chicken stock base)
2 tablespoons flour
1 cup light cream
Salt and pepper
1 dozen eggs, hard-cooked, shelled, and
    sliced crosswise
1 can (4 oz.) green chilies, seeded and diced
1 cup diced sharp Cheddar cheese
½ cup diced Teleme (or jack) cheese
Paprika (optional)

Sauté the chopped onion and rice in 4 tablespoons of the butter until the onion is limp. Add 3½ cups of the chicken stock, cover and cook until the rice is done, about 20 minutes.

Meanwhile, make sauce by melting remaining 2 tablespoons butter in a pan and blending in flour. Slowly stir in cream and remaining 2 cups chicken broth and continue to stir and cook until thickened; add salt and pepper to taste; allow to cool.

Arrange about half the cooked rice in a greased 3½-quart casserole (or two 2-quart casseroles), top with half the egg slices, half the diced chilies, and half of each of the cheeses. Spoon half the sauce over the top; then repeat the whole process. Bake, uncovered, in a moderately hot oven (375°) until bubbly. Garnish with a sprinkling of paprika, if desired. Makes 10 to 12 servings.

Sopa Seca de Tortillas: tortilla strips and cheese arranged in layers and topped with a seasoned sauce.

Sopa Seca de Tortillas

This spicy Mexican dish, rich with cream and cheese, calls for a simple green salad and a light fruit dessert.

1 package (1 dozen) tortillas
⅓ cup lard or shortening
1 cup minced onion
2 tablespoons lard or shortening
4 canned green chilies, seeded and minced
1 cup whipping cream
1 cup tomato purée
Salt
½ pound shredded jack cheese
2 tablespoons butter

Cut tortillas in thin strips with scissors or a knife. Sauté them in ⅓ cup lard until crisp, but do not brown. To make sauce, sauté onion in 2 tablespoons lard until transparent; add chilies, cream, and tomato purée. Simmer for 10 minutes; add salt to taste. Grease a 2-quart baking dish and cover bottom with half the tortilla strips. Pour over half the sauce and add a layer of half the shredded cheese. Repeat layers, ending with cheese. Dot with butter and bake in a moderate oven (350°) for 30 minutes. Makes 6 servings.

Casseroles for a Crowd

Guest meals made easy

Turkey Noodle Casserole

You need to cook the noodles just before assembling and heating this casserole. Things you can do ahead are to roast the turkey and remove meat from bones, make broth, and make the sauce.

18 to 20-pound turkey (including giblets), roasted and cooled
Water (optional)
Salt
½ cup (¼ lb.) butter or margarine
1 large onion, finely chopped
2 cups finely chopped parsley
1¼ cups unsifted all-purpose flour
8 cups (2 qts.) canned or freshly made chicken broth, or turkey broth
4 cups (1 qt.) light cream
1½ cups dry white table wine (or light cream)
2 cans (6 or 8 oz. each) mushroom pieces, drained
6 cups (1½ lbs.) shredded Parmesan cheese
2 pounds spaghetti or tagliarini, boiled and hot

Peel skin from roasted turkey and strip meat from bones. Cut meat in slivers and set aside. If you wish, make turkey broth by boiling bones and skin in 2 quarts water seasoned with 2 teaspoons salt. Pour through wire strainer and reserve; discard bones and skin.

In a large pan (at least 8-quart size for sauce alone, or twice as big to hold turkey and noodles, too) melt butter and add onion and parsley; cook until vegetables are limp. Blend in the flour and gradually add the broth, cream, and wine. Bring to a boil, stirring frequently, and let simmer for about 10 minutes. Stir in the mushrooms and 3 cups of the cheese. (You can make the sauce a day ahead and chill, covered; reheat before using.)

Add turkey and noodles to hot sauce and mix well. Season to taste with salt; if you used the broth made from the turkey bones seasoned with 2 teaspoons salt, you may need 1 to 2 additional teaspoons salt.

Divide the turkey mixture among 2 or 3 large baking pans (such as the bottoms of broiler pans). Sprinkle the tops of the casseroles evenly with remaining 3 cups of cheese. Bake in a hot oven (400°) for 20 to 25 minutes, or until bubbling and top is lightly browned. Makes about 8 quarts, 30 to 35 servings.

Hominy-Chili Casserole

2 large cans (1 lb., 13 oz. each) whole white hominy, drained
3 tablespoons grated onion
1½ cups sour cream or cream sauce
1½ cups coarsely shredded jack cheese
6 canned peeled green chilies, rinsed of seeds, cut in small pieces
Salt to taste
½ cup fine dry bread crumbs, mixed with 3 tablespoons melted butter

Mix hominy carefully with onion, sour cream or cream sauce, jack cheese, green chilies, and salt to taste. Put into a 2½ or 3-quart casserole, sprinkle the top with buttered bread crumbs, and bake, uncovered, in moderate oven (350°) about 30 minutes, or until heated through. Set under the broiler to brown top. Makes 12 servings.

A hearty casserole of golden brown chicken pieces and choice vegetables, baked in wine and judiciously seasoned with herbs, is certainly guest fare. This is Chicken Basque (recipe on page 90).

Chicken Basque

This hearty casserole combines browned chicken quarters with a blend of vegetables and herbs in white wine.

3 broiler-fryers (2 to 2½ pounds each),
   quartered
½ cup flour
2 teaspoons salt
1 teaspoon coarse ground pepper
¼ teaspoon chili powder
½ cup olive oil or salad oil
10 small white onions, sliced
1 clove garlic, minced
½ pound fresh mushrooms, sliced
2 green peppers, cut in long strips
2 small eggplants, peeled and cubed
2 bay leaves
1 tablespoon salt
2 teaspoons thyme
2 teaspoons basil
1½ cups white wine
4 tomatoes, or 1 can (1 lb., 12 oz.)
   whole tomatoes, drained
Salt and pepper

Coat chicken quarters with mixture of the flour, 2 teaspoons salt, pepper, and chili powder; brown in oil in large frying pan. (Use two frying pans to save time.) Remove browned chicken and arrange it in bottom of large casserole, 8 quarts or larger. In same pan, lightly brown onions, garlic, mushrooms, pepper, and eggplant. Arrange browned vegetables around chicken pieces, add bay leaves, and sprinkle with 1 tablespoon salt, thyme, and basil. Rinse frying pan with wine, scraping well. Pour wine over vegetables; cover and bake in moderate oven (350°) for 1½ hours. After 1 hour, arrange tomato quarters over the top, sprinkle with salt and pepper, and cook for the last 30 minutes. Makes 12 generous servings.

Hot Crab Soufflé

You'll need to begin preparation for this shellfish soufflé the day before serving. Accompany it with a citrus salad and hot butter rolls

8 to 10 slices white bread
2 cups flaked fresh crab
1 cup mayonnaise
1 small onion, chopped
1 cup chopped celery
1 medium-sized green pepper, chopped
1 tablespoon minced parsley
1 teaspoon grated lemon peel
1 teaspoon salt
¼ teaspoon pepper
4 eggs
3 cups milk
1 can (10½ oz.) mushroom soup, undiluted
Grated Parmesan cheese
Paprika

Dice 4 slices of the bread and place in bottom of buttered 3-quart shallow casserole, preferably rectangular. Mix together in large bowl the crab, mayonnaise, onion, celery, green pepper, parsley, lemon peel, salt, and pepper. Arrange over the bread mixture.

Trim crusts from remaining slices of bread and arrange over crab mixture to cover completely.

In separate bowl, slightly beat the eggs, add the milk, and beat until well blended; pour over bread. Cover and place in refrigerator overnight. Bake, uncovered, in moderately slow oven (325°) for 1 hour, 15 minutes. Heat soup until just hot; spoon over baked soufflé. Sprinkle generously with cheese; place under broiler for about 2 minutes. Sprinkle with paprika and serve. Makes 12 servings.

Italian-Style Macaroni Casserole

This macaroni casserole is an excellent choice if you're serving a large group. It appeals to all ages. Prepare it ahead of time and bake it just before serving.

Ground beef filling:
2 pounds ground beef
2 medium-sized onions, chopped
1 clove garlic, minced or mashed
1 can (3 or 4 oz.) sliced mushrooms, drained
1 can (8 oz.) tomato sauce
1 can (6 oz.) tomato paste
1 cup water
1½ teaspoons mixed Italian herbs
1½ teaspoons salt
½ teaspoon pepper

Sauté ground beef, chopped onions, and garlic in large frying pan (with a cover) over medium heat until crumbly. Add mushrooms, tomato sauce, tomato paste, water, mixed Italian herbs, salt, and pepper. Stir mixture until it is well blended. Cover and simmer gently for 1½ hours.

Spinach filling:
½ cup salad oil
2 packages (10 oz. each) frozen chopped
  spinach, thawed
2 cups soft bread crumbs
½ cup minced parsley
½ cup grated Romano cheese
1 teaspoon rubbed sage
1½ teaspoons salt

In a large bowl, mix together the salad oil, spinach, soft bread crumbs, parsley, cheese, sage, and salt. Stir mixture until it is well blended.

Macaroni filling:
1 pound butterfly or seashell macaroni
Boiled salted water

Cook macaroni in boiling salted water as directed on the package; drain.

To assemble:
Grease a 9 by 13-inch baking pan and place half the cooked macaroni in the bottom. Top with half the spinach mixture and then half the ground beef mixture. Repeat the layers, ending with the meat mixture on top. Bake, uncovered, in moderate oven (350°) for 30 minutes (if refrigerated, bake for 50 minutes). Makes 10 to 12 servings.

Golden Corned Beef Casserole

Here's a flavorful casserole featuring corned beef and cream-style corn.

2 cans (12 oz. each) corned beef, cubed, or
  4 cups cubed freshly cooked corned beef
2 green peppers, chopped
2 large onions, chopped
½ cup (¼ lb.) butter or margarine
2 cans (about 1 lb. each) cream-style corn
1½ cups crushed soda crackers
1½ to 2 teaspoons salt
½ teaspoon pepper
1 tablespoon minced parsley
2 cups milk
5 eggs, slightly beaten
12 green pepper rings
½ pint sour cream (optional)

Sauté the cubed meat, chopped pepper, and chopped onion in butter until browned. Place in a shallow 3 to 4-quart casserole and stir in corn, crushed crackers, salt, pepper, parsley, milk, and beaten eggs. Bake, uncovered, in moderately hot oven (375°) for 1 hour. Arrange pepper rings on top, and place a dollop of sour cream, if used, in center of each ring. Serve immediately. Makes 12 servings.

Meat Ball and Lima Bean Casserole

This dish combines meat balls with lima beans in a sour cream sauce.

3 packages (10 oz. each) frozen limas, thawed
¼ cup (⅛ lb.) butter or margarine
5 slices bread, cubed
¾ cup milk
3 eggs
1½ teaspoons salt
½ teaspoon pepper
2 cloves garlic, mashed
2 pounds ground beef
¾ cup water (or cooking liquid from lima beans)
2 cups sour cream

Cook limas according to package directions; drain, saving cooking liquid; add 2 tablespoons of the butter to the beans. Meanwhile, soak bread in milk in large bowl. Slightly beat eggs with 1 teaspoon of the salt and the pepper, and add garlic. Add to the soaked bread along with ground beef; blend well. Shape meat mixture into walnut-sized balls.

Brown meat balls in remaining 2 tablespoons of butter; transfer to shallow 3 to 4-quart casserole. Pour water or cooking liquid into the frying pan; stir to remove drippings; pour over meat balls. Mix drained limas with sour cream and remaining ½ teaspoon salt; spoon over meat balls and mix gently. Cover and bake in slow oven (300°) for 30 to 35 minutes. (Or refrigerate up to 6 hours, then bake 50 minutes to 1 hour.) Makes 12 servings.

Pasticcio di Polenta (Polenta Pie)

Polenta Pie makes an excellent casserole to serve for a buffet with baked ham, roast capon, or turkey. Make polenta the day before serving.

2 quarts boiling water
1 tablespoon salt
2 cups corn meal, either white or yellow
¼ cup (⅛ lb.) butter
⅓ cup fine dry bread crumbs
1 pound fresh mushrooms, sliced
3 tablespoons butter
Salt
6 tablespoons grated Parmesan cheese
9 tablespoons light cream
Chopped parsley (optional)

To make polenta, add to boiling water 1 tablespoon salt and sprinkle in corn meal. Cook, stirring, until thick. The standard test in Italy is to cook until a wooden spoon will stand upright in the mush. (It can be cooked over hot water, in which case allow 1½ hours.) When the polenta is sufficiently thick, pour it into a buttered 3½ or 4-quart round casserole, one in which the finished dish may be served. Chill thoroughly.

When ready to complete the "pie," turn polenta out of the casserole and slice into four even layers. The easiest way to do this is with a piece of string.

To make the rest of the dish, butter the casserole thickly with the ¼ cup butter and sprinkle with bread crumbs. Put the top slice of polenta in the bottom of the casserole (this top slice was at the bottom of the casserole, so is returned to its original resting place). Spread ⅓ of mushrooms in this layer, dot with 1 tablespoon of the butter, sprinkle with salt and 2 tablespoons of the grated Parmesan cheese, and pour 3 tablespoons light cream evenly over the top.

Add the next layer of polenta and repeat, using half the remaining mushrooms and the same amounts of butter, salt, cheese, and cream. Repeat again, using last of mushrooms. Dot the top layer generously with butter; cover, and bake in a moderate oven (350°) for 1½ hours. Before serving, sprinkle chopped parsley on top, if you wish. Serve piping hot. Makes 12 to 15 servings.

Beef and Noodle Casserole *(see suggested menu below)* ✳

This hearty beef and noodle casserole may be made ahead and reheated at serving time.

1 package (12 oz.) wide noodles
4 quarts boiling water
2 tablespoons salt
1 tablespoon olive oil

Sauce:

1½ cups chopped onion (1 very large onion)
2 cloves garlic, minced or mashed
¼ cup olive oil or salad oil
1½ pounds lean beef, cut in small pieces
   (about the size of filberts)
½ pound chicken livers, cut in quarters
1 can (6 oz.) tomato paste
2 cups water
1 tablespoon minced parsley
1 tablespoon crumbled oregano
¼ teaspoon freshly ground black pepper
2 teaspoons salt
1 cup dry red wine or tomato juice
Additional water (about 1 cup)

Filling:

3 cups cottage cheese
½ to 1 pound ricotta or jack cheese
Salt and pepper

Cook noodles in boiling water to which salt and oil have been added for about 10 minutes, or until just tender. Drain. In large, heavy pan, cook onion and garlic in olive oil until golden; discard garlic. Add beef and livers to onion and brown lightly. Stir in tomato paste, water, seasonings, and wine. Simmer for 2 to 3 hours (the longer the better), adding more water if necessary. When sauce is done, taste and correct seasoning.

Grease a 3½ or 4-quart casserole. Arrange a layer of noodles in bottom. Cover with layer of sauce, then put spoonfuls of cottage cheese and slices of ricotta cheese on top; sprinkle cheeses with salt and pepper. Repeat until casserole is filled, reserving a few of the noodles for the top; arrange these symmetrically, either as the spokes of a wheel or in a lattice design. Before serving, put in moderate oven (350°) and bake, uncovered, for 45 minutes, or until hot. If casserole is refrigerated, add 30 minutes to the oven time. If noodles on top dry out too much, brush with a little milk or cream. Makes 12 to 16 servings.

✳ Simple Patio Supper

Beef and Noodle Casserole *(see recipe above)*
Mixed Green Salad with Broccoli
Hot Buttered French Bread
Strawberry Shortcake

This is an ideal menu to serve out-of-doors. The casserole is a hearty one. It may be made ahead and reheated at serving time.

Mixed Green Salad with Broccoli

Use the tender tops from 4 pounds of fresh broccoli (or use 4 packages frozen broccoli), and cook them until tender-crisp. Combine with 2 heads romaine, broken in pieces, ½ cup minced green onions, and 2 heads iceberg lettuce. Dress with French dressing. Makes 12 servings.

Strawberry Shortcake

Use a 4-cup recipe for sweetened baking powder biscuit shortcake. Roll thin and cut in 24 circles. Brush 12 of the circles with melted butter, and top with remaining ones. Bake at 450° for 20 minutes, or until nicely browned. Mash, slice, and sugar 4 boxes strawberries. Split shortcakes; put sliced sugared berries between layers and on top. Serve with whipped cream. Makes 12 servings.

Western Cassoulet

2 pounds dry white (Great Northern) beans
Water
1 tablespoon salt
1 teaspoon pepper
1 ham shank, with meat on it
1 medium-sized onion, stuck with 6 to 8
   whole cloves
1 carrot
6 to 8 sprigs fresh parsley
Handful of celery leaves
1 bay leaf
6 pieces each chicken legs and thighs
2 pounds lean pork loin or rib chops
About ⅓ cup bacon drippings, melted butter,
   or salad oil
3 large onions, chopped
2 cloves garlic, minced or mashed
1 pound garlic sausages
2 cups coarse dry bread crumbs
3 tablespoons melted butter

Soak beans overnight in water to cover (or cover with water, bring to a boil, simmer for 2 minutes, then soak for 1 hour). Without draining them, put beans into a large kettle with salt, pepper, ham shank, onion stuck with cloves, carrot, parsley, celery leaves, and bay. Add water, if needed, to cover beans about ½ inch. Bring to a boil, reduce heat and simmer slowly until beans are somewhat more than half done, about 1 hour. (Add more water, if needed to keep beans covered.) Remove ham shank, discard bone, cut meat into bite-size pieces and reserve. Discard seasonings: onion, cloves, carrot, parsley, celery, and bay.

While beans are cooking, arrange chicken pieces and pork chops in a large, greased broiler pan; they should be close together, and in a single layer in the pan. Brush with part of the drippings or melted butter. Broil slowly with the meat about 8 inches from heat for 25 to 30 minutes, or until browned. Turn, brush again with the fat, and continue broiling for 15 to 20 minutes. Set aside the browned meat, drain fat into a frying pan; add onion and garlic to the pan and sauté until soft. Drain the liquid from the beans into the broiler pan and scrape up all the browned particles. Stir onion mixture into the drained beans. Cut sausages into 1-inch pieces. Cut pork chops to make about 12 pieces.

To assemble, spoon a layer of beans and onions into the bottom of a 5 or 6-quart casserole. Cover with about half the pork chops, chicken pieces, ham, and sausage. Add a second layer of beans, then a layer of the remaining meat pieces. Make a top layer with the remaining beans. Pour in the liquid from the broiling pan and add water, if needed, to bring liquid to about ¼ inch below top level of beans. Mix the bread crumbs with the 3 tablespoons melted butter and sprinkle on top of the bean layer. Cover tightly and bake in a moderate oven (350°) for 30 minutes. Remove cover and bake for about 30 minutes longer, or until top is browned. Put cover back on as soon as you remove the casserole from the oven. Wrap tightly in several layers of newspapers and put into a corrugated box to carry to the picnic. Makes 12 servings.

Spinach Custard

Three different cheese flavors are blended in this spinach casserole.

4 medium-sized onions, chopped
2 cloves garlic, minced
½ cup salad oil
4 packages (10 oz. each) frozen chopped spinach
12 eggs
2 teaspoons salt
½ teaspoon pepper
4 cups shredded medium-soft jack cheese
2 cups shredded sharp Cheddar cheese
1 cup cottage cheese

Cook onions with garlic in salad oil until vegetables are soft. Add spinach and cook over low heat until thawed, breaking spinach block apart to hasten heating. Meanwhile, beat eggs until foamy; season with salt and pepper. Stir in jack cheese, Cheddar cheese, and cottage cheese. Combine with spinach mixture. Turn into 2 casseroles (2-quart size) and bake, uncovered, in hot oven (400°) for 40 minutes, or until very softly set; stir 4 or 5 times while baking. Makes 16 servings.

Index

Photographers: Glenn M. Christiansen, pages 4, 84; Darrow M. Watt, pages 1, 7, 10, 13, 19, 20, 22, 32, 35, 36, 40, 44, 58, 61, 71, 74, 78, 81, 87, 88. **Illustrated by** Suzanne Mathison. **Cover photograph:** Beef Burgundy, page 7. Photograph by Darrow M. Watt.